REFLECTIONS
OF HOPE AND LOVE

BY LUKE JOHN GASPARRE

ABOUT THIS BOOK

These words of wisdom will provide you with guidance and insight into your mind and soul. Each written essay will enlighten you and will relate to your inner feelings to make you realize what is real and important in your life. These words will create an inner sense of peace and harmony, making you appreciate all that you have and what others do not possess.

The book is divided for your convenience into separate sections based upon the topics and issues most important to you. This material will be a helpful tool to rectify any kind of setback that you experience on your journey in life. The beautiful poems in the "Romance" section will give you a sense of what love is and what love can be. Being in love is such a special feeling, and these inspirational words will give you insight into your own relationship and make you appreciate how special your love is.

With each reading, you will gain additional knowledge and vision into who you are and who you wish to become. As you incorporate each theme into your mind, you will immediately become aware of the beauty and the deep meaning each one conveys, which will give you a passionate desire to fully understand that it is ultimately up to you to find true happiness.

CONTENTS

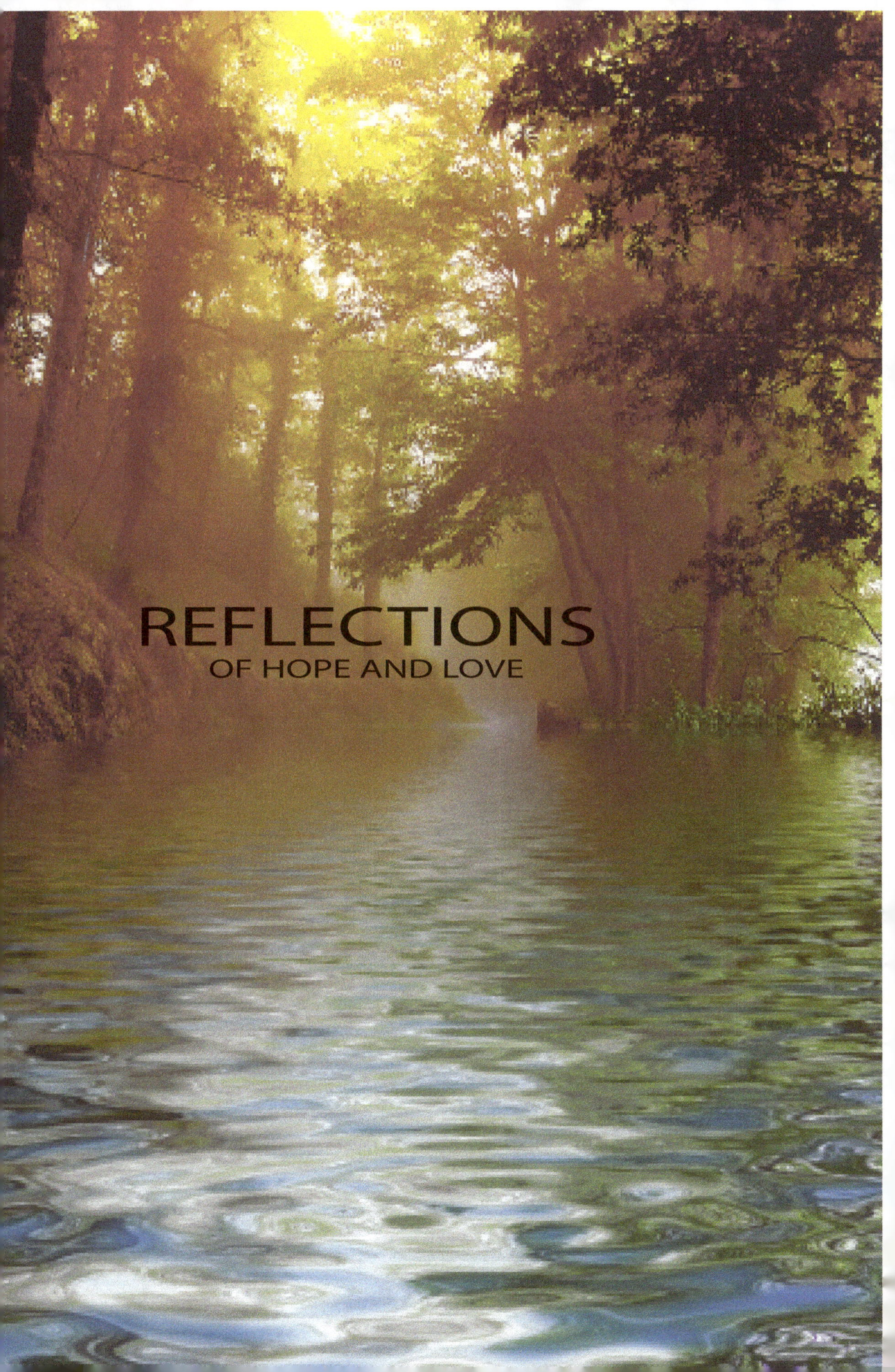
REFLECTIONS
OF HOPE AND LOVE

I

Romance

A Vision of You

As I move across the blue ocean, I see a bright star and a vision of you. The waves are gentle beneath me; they caress me, though they are few.

The shore behind me is no more, and the star above has disappeared. I realize I have lost you, and I become full of fear.

The gentle waves erupt, and I am tossed from side to side. The vision I seek is nowhere to be found. A fury has overwhelmed me, and there is no place to hide.

I know the clouds will scatter, and my star will reappear. I must find a way to rise above and conquer my fear.

Hope was the answer; although I could not see you, you were always there.

Being Faithful

When I spend time with you, my mind is at peace, knowing that our hearts are one. When I'm away from you, it is like I never left because of the faith I have in you. This feeling we have for each other will be cherished for a lifetime because of the commitment and bond that we created with each other. When I am with you, it is like the first time we met, and I hope you feel the way I do because I still love you so.

Because

I love you because you were always there for me when I was down and discouraged.

I love you because you do not judge me but love me.

I love you because you accept me for who I am.

I love you because you are a beautiful human being.

I love you because you are there when I need you.

I love you because I do not like to sleep alone.

I love you because you help me resolve my problems.

I love you because you nurture my soul.

I love you, and I don't want to lose you.

Missing You

I could see my world in your eyes the first time I looked into your soul, felt your love, and realized how much you mean to me. I look toward the future and imagine how our intimate compassion will allow us to become one. When I lie in bed at night, I drift into your world knowing I cannot live without you. In my heart I made a promise to love, protect, and honor you all the days of our lives. You are an inspiration to me and my strength in this world. again.

The Power of Love

He is driven by a deep lust for her but does not know how to satisfy the desires and passions in his heart and soul. He craves a deep connection with her so she can feel the power of his love. It was not until he awoke in her arms that morning that he felt a strong sexual bond that caused him to fall in love.

Your Gentle Touch

I want to be loved by you and made to feel special. I need you to touch me so gently that I can feel your heart next to mine. When I am with you, I am falling more in love with you as we grow closer together. I wish to live the rest of my life with you so I can be near to comfort you and share my deepest secrets with you.

A Distant Love

We were younger then and fell in love. It was a brief moment in time. We made one another happy, and life was so simple for us. We became close in body and mind. It felt like our love would last forever, but it was not real love.

I Can Give So Much

I know one day, deep in my heart, I will find that special person who I will care for always. I can give so much to her from my heart and soul only if she knows how much I love her. All I can do is wait for her to come into my life and show me her love for the first time. I have to be strong and believe that I will find true love because now I know how true love feels.

I Will Be There For You

As the wind gently removed the satin sheets from your body, my heart trembled at seeing the most beautiful woman in my life.

The passion I have for you is beyond my control, and I want to show you my love.

I will be there for you whenever you call.

I will be there for you to satisfy your needs.

I will be there for you when you feel sad and lonely.

I will be there for you the rest of your life, and I pray you feel the same way too.

Moment In Time

When I first met you, you were the love of my life. When we embraced for the first time, I didn't want to let you go. I often think about that moment. It was like yesterday when we first met, and I know it was you too. Now there is a void in my life. I'm alone for the first time without you, and it is a challenge for me to be happy again. All that remains are the memories of you and the love we once had.

My Love Is Strong and True

Spring is upon us, and new love blossoms in my heart.

Winter is behind me, and I need to make a new start.

I see your face before me; I long to hold you close.

I know we are apart, but I think of you the most.

As time goes by I miss you more and more.

Your absence has been painful, and I don't know what's in store.

Do not distrust my love for you.

On that you can be sure.

I have waited for some words from you.

My love is strong and true.

You need to tell me that you love me too,

And that our life together can shine anew.

My Love Is Real

When I am away from you, I miss your precious breath against my face. I cannot be apart from your world of unexplored lovemaking. I visualize us being in a warm embrace and never letting go. The beauty in your heart and soul allows me to be part of your sensual journey through life. The feelings I have inside me want you more than ever, and I promise to show you that my love is real.

We Can Last Forever

I want to do everything in my power to draw you closer to me and to show you we can last forever. Although we are different in many ways, our love will bring us closer, and we can last forever. We must never take for granted the bond between us and must always protect and preserve the bond so we can last forever. We can last forever if we choose to.

Our Lives Will Be Joined

Every night when I close my eyes, my body and mind become one, and I desire to explore your innermost passions and fantasies. The thought of feeling your love and kissing your beautiful lips is a gift I cannot live without. The more we are together, our understanding of love grows, and our lives will be joined forever.

Both Our Hearts Are One

When I spend time with you, my mind is at peace, knowing that both our hearts are one. When I'm away from you, it is like I never left because of the faith I have in you. I will cherish this feeling we have for each other. When I am with you, it is like the first time we met, and I hope you feel the way I do because I still love you so.

What Is Left Of Us

When I lie next to you, I think about how you feel about me. For so long, we embraced each other and shared love and affection. You tell me you love me, but each day we become more distant from each other. What is left for us is knowing that our intimacy can grow if we still have the same feelings and desires in our hearts.

The Story In Your Eyes

You know how I feel about you when I look into your eyes and hold your precious body next to mine. I wish time would slow down so I would be able to be with you forever. When I awake with you near me, I look into your eyes, and a new story brings me ever closer to you. Our love will show us the way and keep us together as one.

I Lost So Much Time

Looking back in time at what we had to overcome, I accept now that we were not right for each other. In the beginning, there was so much love, hope, and promise for us, and I believed we could have survived and lasted a lifetime. Now I sit back and realize that I have lost so much time with you that will never come back. I am saddened that we gave up on each other so quickly and hope that our breakup was not a mistake.

How I Feel About You

After all this fighting, you know how I feel about you. I think I should walk away for now and let you have your way. But there is not enough time to show you what is inside to make you see it my way. Our love should be forever, and you must not break my heart and leave me. I want to feel you and hope you never let me go because I still love you so.

You Left Me In Tears

You left me in tears, and now my life must start over again. You turned your back on me when I needed you most. What happened to us that you couldn't take me back? In the past few nights, deep down inside, I have realized that we were not honest and truthful with each other. I understood that our love was not meant to be when I desired you more than you desired me.

Loving Both Of You

In my life, I never dreamed that I could fall in love with both of you. I am torn by divided love and know I must choose between two beautiful women to end my uncertainty and agony. I do not wish to hurt either one of you and hope you will understand the pain and suffering that I have endured for so long. I struggle within my heart to find my way, knowing that in time your pain will come to an end, and your life can find a new beginning.

A World Without You

We were meant to last a lifetime and share our dreams together.
There are many questions that will never be answered. We never
took the time to start a life together and emotionally fall in love. I
made a promise that I would understand your needs and wishes
for you to be alone in your thoughts. What can I do to make it right
again? I belong in your arms even if it's for one moment. This chance
to love was taken from us, and this caused our relationship to break
apart. Was there anything I could have done to have you come
running back to me? I must find myself in a world without you.

One Last Chance

Why couldn't you give me one more chance and let our love
survive? What did I do to hurt your feelings, to cause you to question
my love? How did you lose trust when we worked so hard to build
our lives together? I know we still have hope, and I don't want to
lose you. One day we will understand that we had one last chance
to come together and learn how to forgive, show respect, and love
each other.

Separate Ways

My life is torn between a world where you are with me and a
world without you. Part of me embraces your spirit. Another part is
tempting me to set your spirit free. We are on a path of uncertainty,
and we failed to protect our love. Spending time alone, we drifted
apart and lost touch with each other. The hopes and dreams we once
had are a distant memory now, and our lives must go separate ways.
Tomorrow will come, and you will be forgotten. Only love can turn
our world around. Just let it be.

You Are The Only One For Me

When you look at me, I keep believing in you and wishing I can take your pain away. Sometimes my words fail to express how I really feel about you when we are close with each other. You are the only one for me, and I will always be there for you. I hope you feel the same way and you can see that we were truly meant to be.

When We First Met

The first time I laid my eyes upon you, I knew I had to spend my life with you. From a distance, your beauty brought me close to you, and I hoped only that you felt the same way too. The thought of you loving me forever brings me great pleasure. You came to me for a short time with great love and passion, and I will never forget when we first met.

Something Special About You

I will always be by your side through your lonely days and nights to guide and support you. You are my dream come true, and I want to become part of your dreams too. We were both given a special gift of love, and we must protect what has been given to us. When I hold you in my arms, there is something special about you that brings me ever closer to the person I cherish and love.

Heart Broken

At this time in my life, I realize how much you mean to me, and my life will never be the same without you. We worked so hard to build a life together, and now it pains me that we are no longer friends and lovers. We discovered our intimate respect for each other only to become heartbroken by our ignorance and pride. We had two different visions of love, and this caused our feelings to change. I will suffer for so long because I still love you and I know that you no longer love me.

The Wrong Person

I ask myself, "Why did this happen to me? Why can't I be with the one I truly love and desire? Why can't destiny bring us together although I know it's wrong?" Our feelings are not equal, my love is not true, and I am thinking of another whenever I'm with you.

I want to break away, but it seems so hard to do. I know I should tell you, but I don't want to hurt you. I ask myself, "What should I do?" As time goes by, I fear I will lose you because of the distance between us and the love that is not possible for us to share. I will always have feelings in my heart for you because I have desired you for so long. All I can do is hope that one day you will love me as I love you.

Touching You

During difficult times I need to reach out to find love. It's been a long time since I had someone by my side. Touching you brings joy and passion to my soul, and I never want to let you go. I wish this feeling between us would last a lifetime, and I hope you feel the same way I do. All I think about is being with you and wishing these feelings would stay alive in our hearts forever.

My Future With You

When I look into the deep blue sky, I see beyond the sun and the stars a world where we can grow and show our love forever. Our days together will last a lifetime and will bless us with an everlasting bond filled with love and passion. When we are together, there is no sense of time, and I want only to be with you. There is nothing that can tear us apart and keep us from each other.

You Are Like An Angel To Me

I can give you so much, and you can give me all that I need to bring a better life back to us. I want to fulfill you; I want to be with you and see you every day. You are mine, and there is no way that I can live another day without you. I want to hug you and make you feel as a woman should feel and not deny you. I desire to be part of you, you are like an angel to me and I can imagine what I can see if only you come to me.

Feelings Of Love

I reflect upon my love life and accept that the feelings I encounter will create intense desires, emotional fulfillment, and happiness blessed with passionate love. There will be times of disappointment and sorrow in my soul. I fear that all hope will be lost and love will be a distant memory. I know there will be many nights I stay awake thinking, "If I would have done things differently, would I still be in love today?" In time, with faith and courage, I can overcome my pain and suffering to love again.

Never Look Back

It doesn't matter what you say because I still love you each and every day. I belong to you for reasons deep within our hearts, and I know in time we both can heal and never look back. We have been through a lot, and we have prevailed and renewed everything that we have given to each other.

Special Moments Together

When I think of the times we spent together, it brings me closer to you because those were special moments we shared. I will hold those memories deep inside my soul as I travel through life. When the days go by and I'm not with you, I think of the memories we share, but I'm fearful of losing you as a friend and a person I truly want in my life. After all the deep moments of sharing happy and sad times, I suffered many long hours thinking that this could not be true and that our circumstance would not allow us the chance to learn and explore our innermost thoughts and desires.

All Because Of You

I never thought I could fall in love again, but I did. I had many chances to find love, but my heart and soul could not be satisfied. My life was going in circles, and I was tired of trying to give myself to another. Being constantly discouraged caused me to feel alone and rejected, without any hope of loving again. For so many years, I was alone and silently suffering, wanting to be loved, and part of me never gave up searching for true love. Now I never look back, and it is all because of you that I'll be by your side until the end of time.

It Wasn't Good Enough

For so many years, my life has been dedicated to the one I love. It was so wonderful that we were given the chance to understand each other and the beauty within us. Since being together with you, my love keeps growing to this day, and I know in my heart we have loved each other with honesty and faithfulness. There was a time when our lack of composure caused us to become distant and question the love that we believed was so strong. The years together were not good enough to preserve all that we had created, and we gave up the hope that we once had.

Tired Of Trying

I don't want to fall to pieces because of you. There is something you need to know before I let you go. I never held you back but always wanted you to grow. Now many things are crashing down upon us, and I am tired of trying. This loss of sleep is too much for me. You were my best friend, and that was a long time ago. I am saddened and disappointed that it had to come to this.

It Doesn't Matter Anymore

All the love I had for you was not enough to see us through. When you looked at me, I believed in you and trusted in your love for me. You had doubts about us, and this caused us pain and uncertainty. Where did we go wrong to make us lose faith in each other? It doesn't matter anymore because we have lost that special feeling. Now our lives will go their separate ways, and all we have left will be our memories.

A Passionate Love

When I fell in love for the first time, all I could think about in my life was you and how I could make you happy. I want to hold you close to my body and feel your scent next to mine. I envision this close intimacy lasting a lifetime. We need to believe in what we have between us to grow and learn about each other's emotional desires. We must never diminish our passion, and we must accept each other for who we are.

I Tried So Hard

You know how much I tried and how I feel about you. When you look at me, I can feel all of your pain that you have suffered, and I want to show you the way so we can be together again. Believe me when I tell you we can come together and try to love again.

The Sharing of Two Lives

After being with you for some time, I have come to appreciate the sweet bond that has developed between us. To share some precious time with you is beautiful, and we never really know how long this will last. Our special friendship has been a mutual sharing of two lives, and you have given me happiness, which I will always treasure. You have fulfilled me as a man, and you have accepted me to be part of your life. I want you to know that I respect you as a woman, and I hope that by being there for you both physically and spiritually, I have taken some of the pain and hurt out of your life. Although we both have accepted pain and suffering, fate has given us joy and comfort in each other.

A Love Not Returned

When I'm with you, I feel the strong love, and I often wonder if you feel the same way toward me. I desire you more and more each day, even when we are apart from one another. I think of how much we have fallen in love with each other and know that it will never end. Even though I feel this way, there is something missing between us, and this is causing me to doubt that we have a future together. When I embrace you, I can feel the distance between us, and it worries me. There is uncertainty in our lives, and I believe there is still time to recreate the love we once had together. I hope through the test of time and being apart from another that, with hope and prayer, we will be able to love again.

In My Life

You changed my life for the better and gave me hope and joy.
You are the only one for me, and I will always be there to take your
pain away. I need you to come into my world and spend the rest of
your days with me. In my life, we were destined for each other, and
the love between us will never change a thing.

One More Chance

I know I have done you wrong and caused you pain. You know
that my love for you is strong and true. You have every right to reject
my love and to cast me aside, and I will understand I have broken
your heart. Give me just a little more time, and our love will surely
grow. I hope you can see things my way, so just give me one more
chance.

I Saw Your Face

When I saw your face for the first time,

I could not believe my eyes.

Your beauty is beyond compare.

All I could do was stare.

I want to hold you and be right there

To love and caress you all night long.

I Feel Your Body

As I embrace you, I feel your body and soul erupting as we fall into each other's arms. I know your desires, and you know mine. In my weakness I could not control my passion, and I entered into your world. We have become one with each other, lost in our lust.

Light Up the World

As I travel into your world, I become more like you. My life is like a dream come true. Now that we are together as one, we must light up the world to show others the love we share is for all to see. It lies beyond your imagination; it seems too good to be true. But with trust in us, you also may be fulfilled.

Don't Want To Let You Go

As I look into your eyes, your body becomes alive. I want to feel your warm, sensitive skin next to mine. We embrace each other, and our bodies are exposed for us to see. I touch your beautiful skin, and I don't want to let you go. I need to be inside you and to feel your love grow.

Just Give Me A Chance

When you are near me, I envision a sensual encounter. Your scent seduces me, and I cannot control my desires. I search deep for the words to express my feelings, but my fear knows I can't have you. I hope you reach out to me and give me a chance.

Without You

I have cherished the true meaning of love and the happiness it brought me. You have given me so much pleasure that without you I could not survive. Our days together feel like they will never end, and I want nothing more than to live out my life with you. Living with you is one of the most beautiful gifts a man could ever imagine.

When You Are Near Me

I hope you reach out to me and give me a sign to let me know that, perhaps, you feel the same way I do. When you are near me I envision a romantic, sexual encounter. We explore each other deeply; we satisfy our needs. I want to take you higher and show you another way. Just give me a chance, and I will show you the way.

Beauty Within

When I look at you I see the beauty within you that cannot be denied. I want to become a part of you and for us to be in the same place. As I gaze into your eyes, my heart blocks my way. I fear what I see, but your smile teases me and tells me what I have to say.

I Feel You By My Side

I close my eyes and feel you by my side. I see you in my dreams and hear you calling my name. From a distance, your scent brings me closer to you than ever. I desire to taste your love and experience all the pleasures we can enjoy together.

When We Met

The first time I set my eyes upon you, I knew I had to spend my life with you. From a distance, your beauty brought me close to you, and I only hoped that you felt the same way. Thinking of you brings me great pleasure with the thought of you loving me forever. You came to me for a short time with great expectations only to lose you in the end.

When Darkness Comes

When I had my first dream and my last dream, it was all about you and the beautiful person you are to me. I know that you are not in my life and that you are far away, but every night when I close my eyes, I enter into a beautiful dream and see your smile; we are together, if only for a short time. When I close my eyes at night, all I think about is you, and I hope that my dreams come true. I hope the day goes by quickly, so when darkness comes, I can see you again.

Love: What Is It?

Love: what is it? It's not holding hands. It's not a sweet kiss. It comes and goes. Love lives in your heart and will never die. That we know is true. To love someone you must make love and reveal it to the world. Express your love to get it in return. Don't be uneasy to love if you want to receive the love. Do not fear rejection. To grow, open your heart and give a chance to love.

Break Away

I want to break away, but it seems so hard to do. I know I should tell you, but I don't want to hurt you. I ask myself what I should do. As time goes by, I feel I will lose you because of the distance between us and the love that is not possible for us to share. I will always have feelings in my heart for you because I have desired you for so long. All I can do is hope that one day you will love me as I love you.

II

Relationships

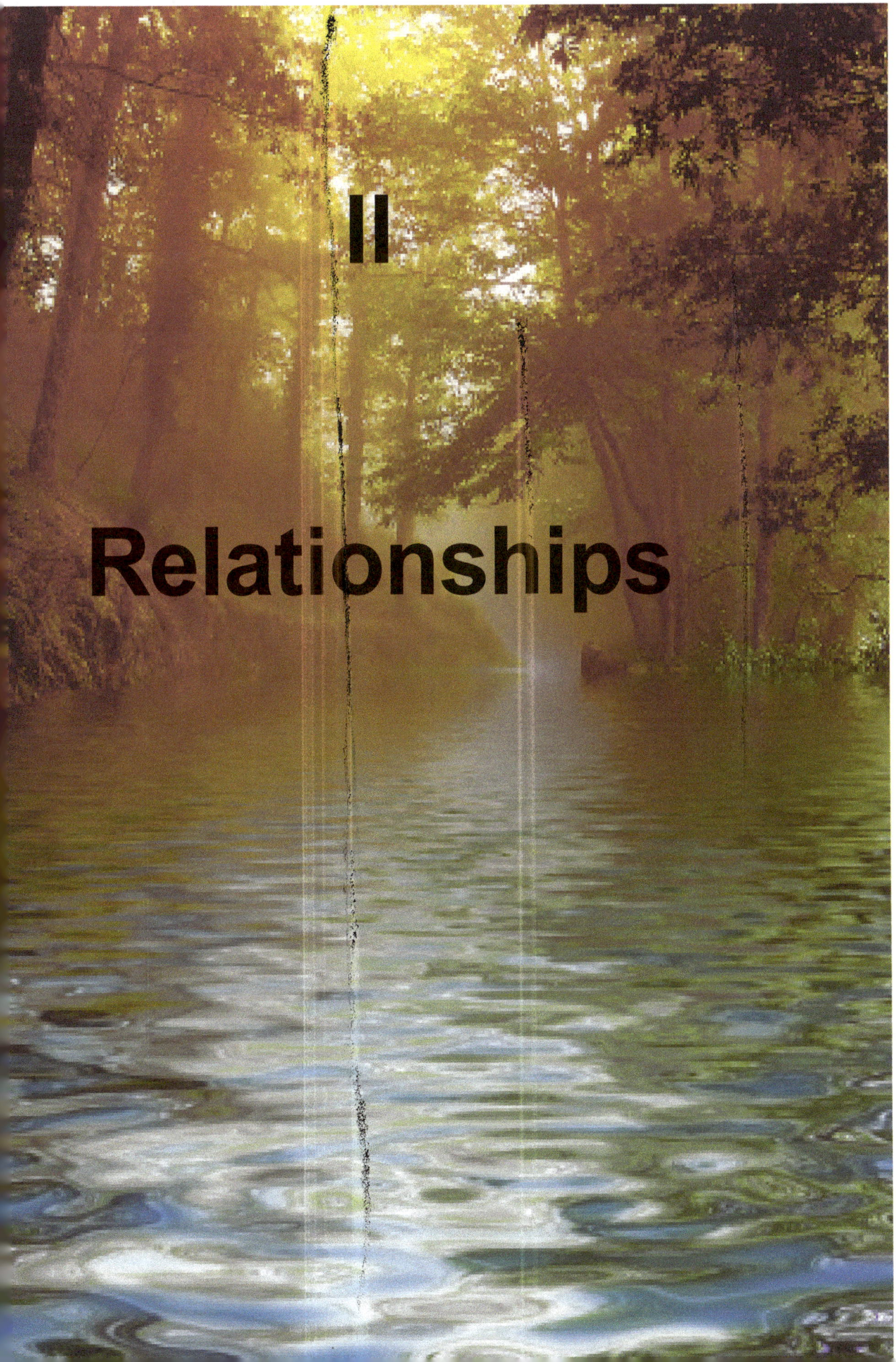

What Is A Friend

A friend is not easy to find. You will know when you have found her. There is an everlasting bond between friends for life. Once created true friendship blossoms for all eternity. With friendship comes respect, happiness and joy. When encountering difficulties in your life a true friend gives you her shoulder to lean on, her ear to listen and her heart to understand your pain.

My Sister, My Love

In my heart and mind, I have been blessed with the good fortune of having a sister to be by my side for a lifetime. When we are happy, we rejoice together, and when we are sad, we bond in sorrow. A relationship with a sister is based upon loyalty, love, and devotion. We learn to accept and understand each other and to preserve this special God-given gift for eternity.

Your Promise To Me

When you give yourself over to someone, you are making a serious vow to love, respect, and support each other's dreams, hopes, and desires. To foster a successful relationship, you must first learn to understand each other and accept each other for who you are and appreciate what comes from the heart and soul. To preserve that intimate trust, you must be conscious of your partner's feelings and do everything that will sustain that beautiful inner sensitivity. Always show kindness, and compliment her beauty to show your commitment and your promise of loyalty forever.

All Alone

I find myself all alone as a single parent, wondering how I will be able to carry on without you and with little hope of finding my way. When we first started our family, I never imagined that I would have the strength and the ability to live a life of loneliness. It seems like a dream that this has happened to me, and I'm struggling to understand the consequences that I face. All I care about is the future for myself and my child, and that nothing tears us apart. I know that the passage of time will soften the pain and give me the strength and the wisdom to overcome a life that I did not chose to live.

My Special Bond

My special friend was a gift that was meant to last a lifetime. We developed a loving relationship that became my source of strength and inspiration to my family. When I face sadness and turmoil, your loyalty comforts me and gives me hope to love again. It would be difficult for me not to have you in my life, and I will suffer for years after you are no longer part of my dreams.

Love Never Gives Up

When you begin to see an emotional change in your relationship and sense that your love is fading, it is time to pause to reflect and understand the reality that confronts you. It is important to reach out to each other and communicate your feelings and your intentions to heal and preserve all that was once a secure and close, loving, passionate bond. We must always find the way to renew our love and forever show compassion, affection, and gratitude for each other. When you follow your true feelings, you will last a lifetime together.

My Brother, My Leader

A relationship with a brother is a source of strength and a commitment to have and protect one another for all infinity. It is built upon trust and friendship toward each other, and it is designed to form a perfect harmony and everlasting joy. This connection with a brother will lead to understanding and reaching out when there is a sign of despair or a need to guide the other through leadership.

Believing In Yourself

You must always look forward with your true feelings of desire to preserve all you have accomplished in life. It is so wonderful to imagine how you can be part of your own dreams and to share them with the ones you love. You must continue to search and to never give up on yourself. Remember where you came from; this will make you stronger and emotionally wiser in your quest for happiness. You will accomplish your potential only if you remain true to yourself and be honest in your relationships with others.

Mistakes We Made

When we first met our lives were happy and full of great hopes and dreams for our future. Despite the many hardships that we struggled to overcome, we have triumphed over many challenges. I'm still trying to understand what caused you to walk away when we were so close and full of desire for one another. I may have failed you in many ways, but I will always love you and be there for you when you need me. I will spend the rest of my days alone, waiting for you

to

come back to me.

Father And Child

The relationship between father and child is a special and loving
creation forged with caring, nurturing, and communicating. As
a father, your role is to be a forceful model and teacher of family
values with a deep understanding of the child's needs. It is your
responsibility to appreciate that your tender, loving child completely
relies upon you and has the privilege and honor of having a strong
male figure in his or her life. It is so important for all children to have
a father who will provide spiritual strength and a life that will lead to
happiness and fulfillment of their wishes and aspirations.

Successful Relationships

A successful relationship requires honesty, trust, communication,
and mutual understanding. In everyone's life, relationships are a
priority because they help us grow as an individual and enable us
to learn about ourselves, other people, and the world around us.
They are fragile and must be protected in order for each relationship
to thrive and develop. Your friendship with your family, friends,
and intimate partner is essential for your personal self-esteem and
respect. All of these special relationships bring love, comfort, and
happiness.

Don't Stop Your Love

You need to support each other to make your dreams come true.
Do not suffocate, discourage, or prevent your partner's vision. Show
your interest in her creative ideas, and provide an atmosphere in
which you can bring peace, love, and harmony to each other.

What Is A Good Parent?

A good parent is someone who knows his or her children and has taken on the great responsibility of caring and showing love, affection, and providing moral leadership. When God made your gift of a child, an immediate attachment was created that can never be broken and that strengthens the unity of the family. Parenthood makes it essential for you to ensure the child lives happily in a stable and secure home environment. A child learns and appreciates right from wrong as long as he or she is afforded the opportunity to experience a positive upbringing from both parents, who were blessed with being a mother and father.

Confront The Truth

There will be days when your love will be tested and you will have to confront the truth. It takes two strong individuals to understand and recognize the loss of love that they once shared together. If you have love in your heart, there will be no reason to control and dictate to those you adore and admire. You have to accept each other for who you are and always show admiration and compassion so your feelings for each other will last a lifetime.

She Must Choose

She is experiencing a deep depression since leaving him. She is torn between family and wanting to move on with her life so that she can have a change she desperately needs. She desires the best of both worlds but knows in her heart that she must choose between a relationship and discovering her own happiness.

Looking Within

The more you share with someone, the more compatible your life will be. Looking within another person enables you to perceive his or her world and find a closer, more intimate relationship. This will bring you together and allow you to explore your inner thoughts and feelings. Allowing ourselves to understand and appreciate the gifts we offer each other will create the bond necessary for a continuous life. In life, we strive to create a family full of love and peace.

Meaning Of Love

When you fall in love for the first time, you become one in body and mind, and you understand the meaning of love. Our lives desire the intimacy and passion that only love can bring to keep us together. Each day, our love will call us to explore our physical and spiritual tendencies and will invite us to find new expressions of kindness and pleasure. Once you have bonded in love, your friendship with each other will reveal the true meaning of love.

True Love

What is true love, and how can we attain it? Once you experience the feeling of real love, it is easy to lose it. How do we fulfill the passionate desire for a lifetime? What is required is an understanding of the other person's reality and dreams. When this emotion is accepted, the bond between the two can grow and last forever.

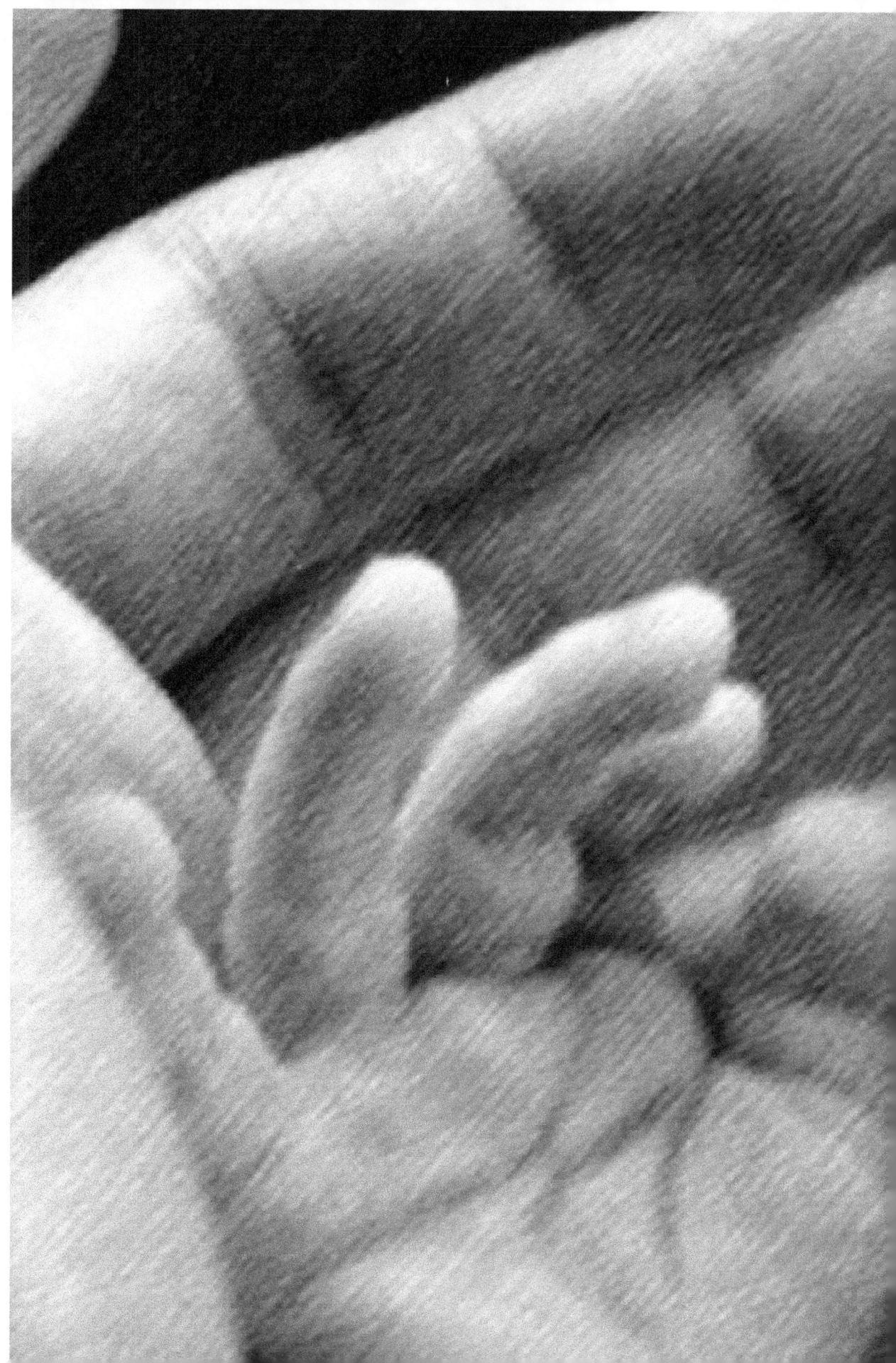

Getting Along

To get along with others, you must strive for peace and harmony with each other and never give up on your quest for true friendship and love. You must appreciate your own feelings and personality, and accept new relationships with the hope of understanding each other. Time spent together must always be meaningful and respectful to enable bonding, and to overcome the many burdens that we will face throughout life. Understanding each other's feelings and desires will have a positive impact on all relationships, hopes, and dreams.

The Beauty Within

Look deep into your soul and you will see beauty all around you. You must look beyond your physical flaws and realize beauty is within. Do not worry about what others have. Focus attention on improving your own qualities, and once you accept this truth, you will feel free from your setbacks and find true happiness in your life.

Intimacy Of Desire

Every time I am with you, my body is addicted to our intimacy of desire. When I embrace you, I imagine our bodies in union with each other, and this feeling grows stronger each and every day. When we are separated, I want you more than ever.

Intimacy Of Trust

When I'm alone and in my deep thoughts, I truly believe that the intimacy of trust will overpower all other feelings. My way of thinking is engulfed by strong temptations and desires for true love and passion. In my heart, I must be aware of how important it is to be honest and truthful in my relationship with my soul mate. We both want our strong, passionate feelings to last a lifetime and preserve the opportunity that was given to us when we fell in love. In your life, being in love is the ultimate of all you can attain, and that feeling of love, if altered, can have a shattering impact on your emotional and psychological well-being. As people, we are gifted with the power to express our thoughts and our pain, and with time, the healing process will allow us to truly understand the intimacy of trust.

Truly Unselfish

She captivates others immediately and accepts them for who they are, and that causes people to recognize the warmth and humanity she so naturally exudes wherever she goes and to whomever she meets. She is a blessing to all who know her. There is something unique in her face and in her eyes that reflects the love and humanity in her heart and that makes her a truly unselfish and dedicated individual to our family.

Desire To Be Successful

If you want to achieve success in life, you must first possess the desire to be successful. With this goal in mind, you must materialize and externalize specific and concrete actions to make your dreams a reality. Always think and make decisions that will not interfere with your journey toward success. Create relationships with those who support your goals. Beware of negative influences that will deter you from your ambitions, and associate with those who are already successful in life.

Second Chance

She looks at you with her sexy eyes and melts your heart away. You know you can't have her, so you look the other way. You may not have a second chance to fall in love, so you must tell her how you feel before she walks away. Find your strength, conquer your fears, and have the confidence to take a chance to fall in love.

The Special Ones

When they come into this world, we expect our children to be healthy and live long, peaceful lives. Unfortunately, some will not have this opportunity to live free from pain and suffering. When a child does not experience the fulfillment and enjoyment of life, it affects not only the child but also all of society. Life is special to all children, no matter what obstacles and burdens they carry. We must always provide love and support to the children with special needs and wants so they can understand and appreciate who they are and why they are the special ones.

It Has Come To This

Why must our lives take us so far apart? We once had a beautiful relationship that brought us closer together and gave us true love and happiness. The feelings that we had were so special and meaningful that nothing could break us apart. As our lives matured, we each took separate paths and grew further apart, and I don't know why. We worked so hard to understand one another and thought our love would never end. We saw the ending coming but did not realize the truth, and it has come to this.

Alone

When I sit alone and think of you and the wonderful days we spent together as father and daughter, my mind goes through so many dimensions that I don't know what's real and what to say. I only know that I don't have you in my life another day. You did not cause this loneliness and pain, but in time, you will understand what this all means. One day you will realize the truth and find the answer to all the confusion that surrounds us. In the end, love will allow us to be together again, and to restore what we once had.

Last Chapter

I have finally realized that I have come to the last chapter in my life and that I have been missing a deep sense of harmony within my soul. I have suffered many disappointments, and I often fear the road ahead. Deep down I know what I want and what I have been missing. I long for a new life full of passion and love with a special person who I can relate to and share the rest of my life with. If given the chance to start a new chapter in my life, I would express the deep love and commitment that I feel for you so that all of your hopes and dreams would come true.

Betrayal

Betrayal is the worst form of violating a sacred trust. It is a breach in the relationship between two individuals who believed in each other and trusted each other. The damage created by betrayal may never be cured once there is a violation of confidence between friends. Your hopes and expectations are severely altered and can be restored only with the passage of time and the building of faith.

A New Beginning

No one could imagine the pain and sense of loss when an innocent child is no longer part of a loving family. There is a special bond that exists between a parent and child, and when that bond is broken by death, the child's life is suddenly altered, and the path to recovery will be a challenge. The road is hard, but with faith in God and confidence in one's own ability, the child will find a new beginning. As a child of God you never walk alone, and one day you will realize the true meaning in your pain.

Broken Hearts

They say that a broken heart can be mended, but if that is true, how is it that so many broken hearts remain in pain? At one time or another you will endure a loss of love and search for an answer to overcome it so you can move on. It will take more than the passage of time to eliminate those thoughts of loneliness and confusion. You will always be haunted by the void in your heart; it will never go away. There is no answer to your pain, but you must gradually accept the loss and move into the future. Do not deceive yourself by thinking you can recreate the past because that is impossible.

Never Love Again

There are many nights I lay awake asking myself where I went wrong with my life and my relationships. I think about us, and I feel I did not deserve this hardship and all the pain and suffering I'm going through. There is a part of me that misses your touch, but deep within my soul I know that in time I will be happier without you. It is difficult for me to think of us because of how deeply I was neglected and betrayed. I know that, for me, it will take time to get over this hurt and to love again. I know now that I can be happy without you and that, in time, I know that you will realize your loss and that you will never find a person like me who loved you in a special, faithful way. I'm saddened and disappointed that we must part and go our separate ways, never to love again.

Fading Away

For many years I had a dream of spending the rest of my life with you and sharing our happiness together. There is nothing wrong with dreaming, but, sadly, I find my dreams of you are fading. For many years we enjoyed each other's friendship and the pleasures of life that brought us closer together as friends and soul mates. Without you there is pain and heartache, and the future is unknown. I'm confused and heartbroken that you left me more than once. As time went by I began to realize there was something missing from my life, and it was passionate love, which I needed to overcome my loneliness. I only hurt myself by staying as long as I did in the hope you would feel the same way about me that I felt about you.

Accepting One Another

When I first fell for you, I thought I knew you.

We grew closer, and we shared precious moments.

But that was not enough.

Our feelings for one another could never come back, and our lives drifted apart.

I Can't Go Back

As much as I love you, I can't go back.

As much as I still desire you, I can't go back.

As we grew together, we grew apart.

Although we shared our love, we seemed like two different people.

As we became closer, there were two different loves: one strong and then the other.

We gave up on one another, and I can't go back.

I Don't Know How

There was so much hope and potential, but I don't know how.

There was so much love, but I don't know how.

There were so many memories, but I don't know how.

So I asked myself how we went wrong?

You No Longer Want Me

As time goes by without you, my feelings for you grow weaker. There is only disappointment now that you have moved on with your relationship, and I finally got the message that you no longer want me to be a part of your life. I will always remember you and think of the happy times we spent together, but now I only have one thing left to say: I hope you are happy, but I will miss you and the memories we share.

You Are My Pet and the Love Of My Life

Since you came into my life, I think of you night and day. You are my pet and my best friend, and I miss you when you go away. We depend on each other, and I will never let you go. The love I have for you is deep and everlasting, and all I want to do is hug and kiss your furry body all day long. I give you my love because you are my reliable friend and companion, and you never let me down. The thought of losing you has an everlasting impact and would change me forever. I pray that you stay healthy, along with me, so we may enjoy each other for years to come.

Part of Your Life

As time goes by without you, my feelings for you grow weaker. There is only disappointment now that you have moved on with your relationship, and I finally got the message that you no longer want me to be part of your life. I will always remember and think of you and all the happy times we spent together, but now I only have one thing left to say: Goodbye forever, my love.

Losing You

There will come a time when I will have to believe it will be hard for me to go on without you. I was not there for you when you reached out to me for some meaning in our lives. I need you near me, and there should be nothing to hide between us. I know we have a chance, but I was afraid of losing you. There's little time left for us to build on what we once had. We must find a way to come closer. It will be hard for me to move on without you, and we must pray and hope we both find true happiness.

The Importance of Beauty

Beauty is so essential to oneself. Beauty has a cleansing quality that touches the body and soul. It makes us who we are and fulfills our innermost desires. There is beauty in all of us, and there is no difference in who you are; always love the beauty within you and let your beauty show. By letting your beauty show and your body glow, you allow the world into your soul to experience your inner love.

Drifted Apart

It didn't have to be this way. I saw from a distance that our love was nearing an end. Every day felt the same, and I became more uncertain and confused about you. We lost so much time when we could have come together as one. But that chance has drifted away, and our feelings no longer keep us together.

It's Time To Let Go

When you realize you are not happy, it is time to let go. When you realize you are not loved, it's time to let go. When you realize you are happy and loved, it is time to embrace it.

.

Come Into My Life

A dream has been born, and two lives have been joined. The bond that we have created for the past nine months will bring us ever closer, and we will grow stronger each day. I have been waiting a long time for you to come into my life so we can share our love and our dreams. You are a gift to me, and I will cherish and guide you all the days of your life.

It Was Not Meant To Be

I shoulder a heavy burden thinking of you. It weakens me that my desire for love cannot be fulfilled. Our friendship was new and exciting, and the memories are everlasting. I controlled my feelings, knowing in my heart that it was not meant to be. We have both experienced pain and suffering in our lives, and in time, your hurt will heal. All I wish is for you is to be happy and find true love. I now know that I must also move on without you and discover happiness with another.

Will Not Let You Go

When you find yourself in love with two women, choosing between them is difficult. The passion within your heart will not allow you to decide. You love them both, and you need them to be a part of your life. They love you equally and will not let you go. Love is so powerful and allows you to love two.

A New Start

Without you in my life, I must make a new start. I look back at what could have been, and this brings pain to my heart. But I understand now that I must figure out who I am and accept who I have become. In time, I will find peace and meet the love of my life.

III

Emotions

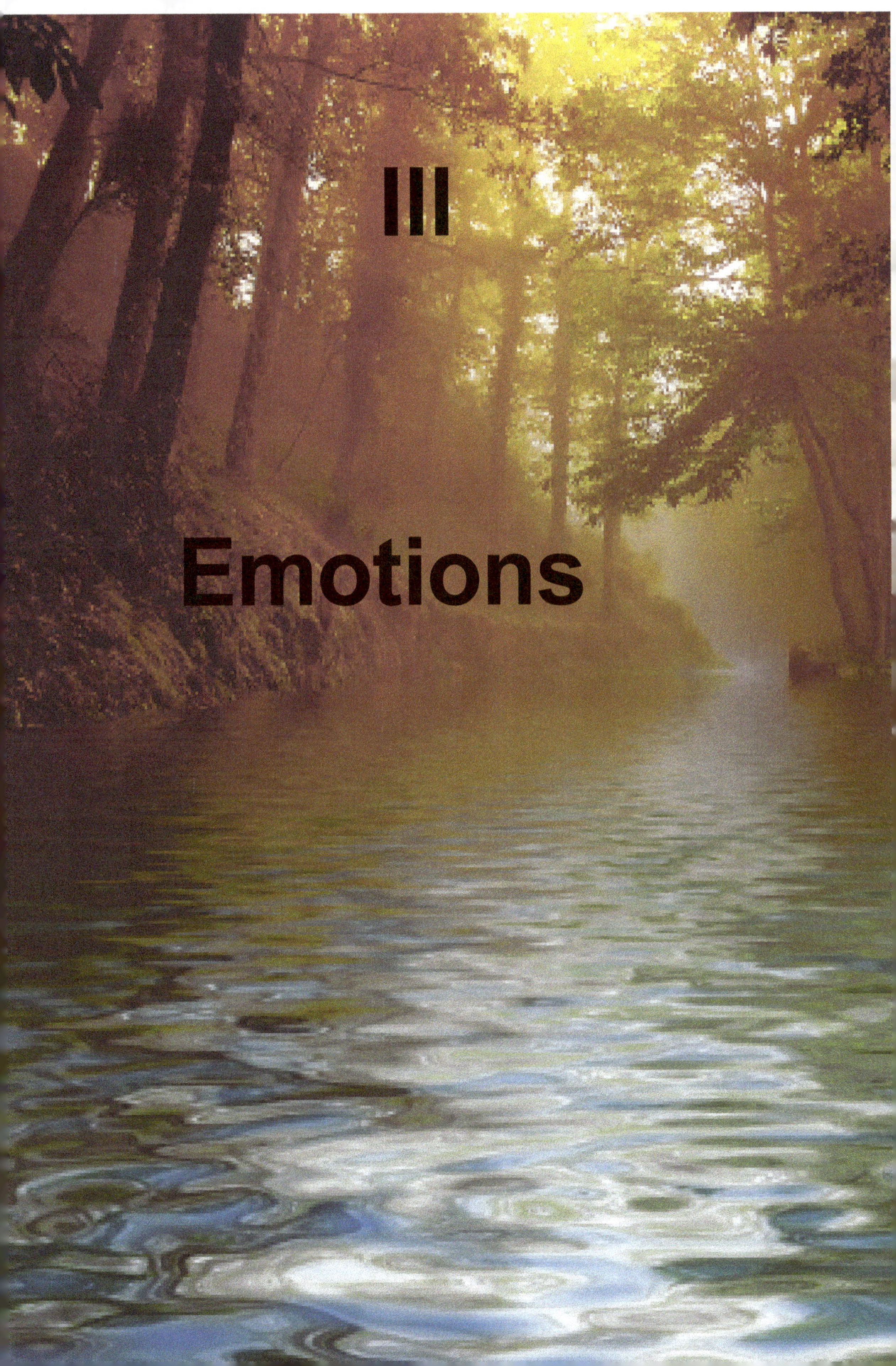

What's In Your Future

When you come into this world the future lies before you.
Filled with hopes and desires, you will be faced with obstacles
and challenges. You have the power to alter the universe and to
experience both successes and failures that may lead to pain at times
and feelings of great accomplishment at other times. The abilities
that you possess come from deep within your mind and soul, and
you will learn about yourself and the world around you. What you
imagine in your heart and soul will become a reality when you truly
believe and appreciate life to its fullest and the gifts you were given.

Don't Look Back

Today, it is raining; tomorrow, the sun will shine. It will be a
new day for you to see all the possibilities within yourself and to
overcome your burdens and fears. Believe in yourself, and appreciate
that there is nothing wrong with feeling down, sad, or confused.
But do not allow these feelings to discourage you or make you lose
hope in yourself. Don't blame yourself for your lack of confidence. Go
forward, and always remember: don't look back at what hurt you in
life

Changes In Your Life

There comes a time in our lives when we search for the answers
that will give us closure to all of our misguided hopes and dreams.
The truth is you cannot change your past but can only alter your
future. So it is upon you not to dwell on your misfortunes but focus
on what you can accomplish for yourself and others. Only when you
realize the changes in your life will you be able to foresee a future
that will bring you success and pleasure.

What Lies Ahead?

When I woke up this morning I had a new vision on life. In the past, life seemed so fruitless and meaningless. I had no feelings or desire to see what lies ahead. I now realize this is my chance to correct and reconcile the mistakes I have made time after time. My life has changed for the better and I feel I have no choice but to forget my past and to build upon my future.

When Life Fails You

When life fails you and you lose hope, you are at a critical point in your life. You need to extinguish the pain you are feeling and the choice is up to you to decide if your life is worth living.

Being unhappy is a normal reaction to the pain you feel. You must believe in yourself and rise above your dilemma. Do not seek answers that will harm you further and cause you added grief. Seek answers that will make a difference in your life and you will be able to see a bright future.

Uncertain Journey

When you have to make a crucial decision that will influence your emotional stability, your mind will become conflicted, causing you uncertainty and confusion. This emotional misery, if allowed to continue, will eventually lead to a more complicated life of suppression. There will come a time during this uncertain journey when you are overwhelmed by a force that must be defeated within your conscious mind. Once you conquer this mental division and believe you have made the right choice, your life will be free from this agonizing mental chaos.

Not About Being Sad or Unhappy

Depression is not only about being sad or unhappy; it is a far worse experience than most people can imagine. It must be recognized as a serious disorder that can have devastating effects for you and your loved ones. For many who suffer from depression, life has become such a burden that it's difficult to confront reality and overcome the confusion in the mind. We all suffer from dramatic consequences that weaken our mental capacity and make it difficult to recognize the demons within us. Seeking love, family, and professional guidance are the necessary first steps in the healing process. We must not fall prey to forces in the mind that test us and tempt us to give up on ourselves. We must stay positive, focus on our happiness, and have faith in ourselves to overcome the depression. We must use our minds not to hurt ourselves but to help ourselves.

The Future Is Now

Your life is like a ticking clock, and whether you realize it or not, your hopes and dreams are passing you by. It is up to you to find a new way to understand yourself. You must live in the present and not in the past. The future is now.

Standing Tall

The challenges that will confront you may darken your strong views about life and the ability to rise above your inner fears. Only you can stand tall and preserve your future for what will become your destiny. You should never give up because time is always on your side, and the strength that you possess will guide you to peace and happiness.

Without Hope

Without hope, you have no chance of ever succeeding. Only you have the power to rise above your despair. The way you look at the world influences your ability to overcome the barriers in your life. You have to believe in yourself and break through negative stereotypes that you and others hold about yourself. Then you must surround yourself with positive role models to provide new opportunities to have faith and belief in yourself.

You Have So Much To Live For

When you are in total despair, not knowing which way to turn, you must realize that life is precious and you have so much to live for. As persons, we desire to live a life free from pain and suffering and wish to live endlessly. Life is short to begin with, and the time that we have to fulfill ourselves is imperfect and full of uncertainty and regrets. The confusion is in your mind, so make the right decisions to help you and persuade your thoughts not to inflict bodily harm or death on yourself. If you confront the demons within yourself, you will understand you have so much to live for.

Be Strong, Be Brave

The mind controls your destiny and visions for your future dreams. You will first have to overcome the obstacles and negativity that will come upon you and seek to drain your opportunity for happiness in life. You must not lose sight of the hope within you and not allow fear to overwhelm you and control your freedom. Be strong and brave, and remember that with time and patience, you will find peace in your soul and love in your heart.

During The Difficult Times

During the difficult times, it is easy to become depressed, dejected, and anxious about the future and what lies ahead for you and your relationships. You must remember not to dwell on past misfortunes and setbacks in your life. There will be times when you will deal with challenges and hurdles that can affect your direction and goals for the future. You must always find strength and meaning to move forward and never look back on what could have been a life full of passion and feeling that you so truly deserve. All you can do now is wait and hope love will come rushing back to you again.

Strength of Character

During your life's journey, you will experience many challenges and setbacks, as well as personal accomplishments. You must have the strength of character to be willing to lose in life. This is not a sign of weakness but rather an opportunity to grow and understand your capability to rise above your limitations. Life involves winning and losing, and you will be able to distinguish between the two and prevent failures in the future. Time and experience will help prevent you from repeating past errors and bad decisions and allow you to reset your life once again.

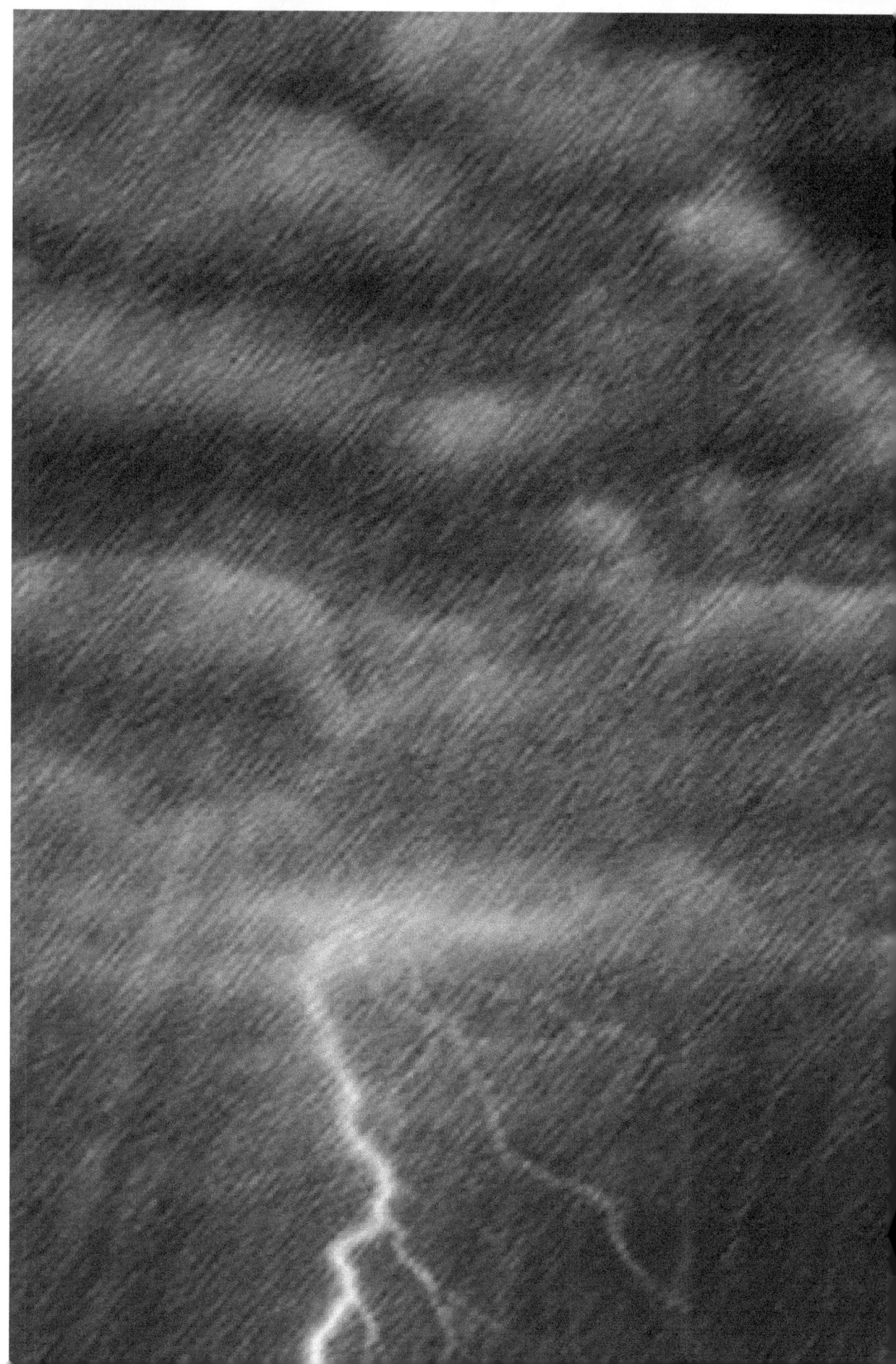

The Conflict Within You

You have two dimensional minds to resist the constant temptations and resentments directed against you by those who intend to harm and damage your inner emotional strength. There will come a time in your life when you will come to the decision to resign yourself and have little faith in your heart. Your mind is torn between doing what is right and wrong. You will spend many hours with this emotional conflict, causing you confusion, stress, and inaction. In the end, after so many puzzling thoughts, you say to yourself, "I truly made the wise choice in life. And now I am able to go forward with a clear vision and can understand with time that the conflict within me has relieved my sorrows."

A New Day

Lying in bed at night, a peaceful feeling comes over me, and my mind is set free from all the chaos and troubles that plague me day in and day out. As the new dawn appears, I begin to realize the uncertainty and fear that may overcome me. I look all around and see a world not meant for me. I will not be discouraged because I know I need to change the way I look at things. I hope to find a way to be part of this strange new world that frightens and confuses me. For now, I will focus on the future and make the world and me come together as one.

Believe In Yourself

You will succeed only if you truly believe in yourself and love who you are. Never give up faith in yourself, and remember that you will reach your goals and will prosper in time. Recognize your skills and abilities, and do not be tempered by those who seek to place obstacles on your path to happiness. Be vigilant and suspicious of your surroundings at all times, and do not let negative thoughts influence you.

Fear In My Life

In my life, I find it difficult to see a meaningful place for me in the world. I search deep within my soul, but I am unable to find myself in this strange and confusing life. My remaining time is growing too short, so I must discover a different path to my salvation. Imagine when you have no hope, and every day is filled with despair and a desire to live no more. What I feel and what I need to do must come together to empower me to overcome the fear that has been with me for so long.

Remain True To Yourself

You must always look forward with your true feelings of desire to preserve all you have accomplished in life. It is so wonderful to imagine how you can be part of your own dreams and to share them with the ones you love. You must continue to search and never give up on yourself and remember where you came from. This will make you stronger and wiser in your quest for happiness. You will accomplish your expectations only if you remain true to yourself and be honest in your relationships with others.

Hardship Beyond Control

When hardships beyond our control multiply and the mind loses command of reality, we become vulnerable to a fall into the unknown world of nonexistence. Life becomes a mere shadow of broken images, and it clouds our mind and spirit. It disintegrates before our very eyes into fragments of what was once a beautiful and supportive foundation. Lives are spiraling downward into a boring and repetitious cycle of meaningless gestures and little respect.

The Mirror

When I look at myself, what do I see? Am I merely a reflection, or is this really me? As I keep looking, a new image appears, and it's not who I am. I feel differently now that I have recognized my true self, and this has caused me to accept who I am.

Despair

When you find yourself in times of despair, you must reach down deep in your soul to fight that feeling of hopelessness in your life. You must realize that life is so precious and given to us as a gift from God. To give up on your own life is such a sad and unjustifiable act of selfishness. Remember, there is always hope in the future and always someone who is suffering too. Accept that you are not by yourself in a world where there is so much despair.

Understanding My Crisis

Upon learning of my sickness, I asked, "Why me?" My life has dramatically changed, and now I sit in silence, trying to understand my crisis that I am determined to accept and to prepare myself for an uncertain future. This conflict within me strengthens my conviction to carry on and move forward with my life. I must be brave and possess the will to fight the odds against me, and this will bring peace and closure to my close friends and beloved family.

You're Not Alone

When we suffer a traumatic loss, we often feel alone and without hope. The world seems dark with very little assurance, but we must not fear because we are not alone. Others experience the same fate. Upon learning of a tragic discovery such as a sudden accidental death or a long-term illness, we are not alone. So we must never forget that no matter what cross we bear, our deepest memories will keep us strong and alive and give us strength to face new challenges.

Preserving Your Happiness

In my mind I think of the most important thing in the world, which is to preserve the happiness I possess in myself and how I would be able to fulfill the happiness of another person. I know I must never give up in my quest to achieve perfect love and harmony and in the end; I will be a better person for others. When your heart and spirit are full of happiness and desire this will help you reach your goals of joy, peace and composure.

Forever By Yourself

When you have dislike in your heart, you are forever alone in anger and misery. This deep obsession will take your life into a shadow of darkness, and you will be unable to rise above your emotional hatred. This fear of being alone will cause deep depression within you and expose you to a world of nonexistence and uncertain behavior. If you allow yourself to remain in this mental hysteria, your chances of survival will be greatly diminished, and you will distance yourself from society and give up the life that you had once before.

Lost In My Thoughts

As I walked through the park without you, I was on the road to nowhere with no path in sight. I was trying to unravel my innermost thoughts, but that feeling of loneliness would not set me free. I felt my life slipping away; the days felt like years without you. I have no more tears to shed for you, and I have come to the end of my feelings for you. There is nothing that can keep us together, and I am lost in my thoughts forever.

The Less Fortunate

In my life, I am fortunate to have someone who loves and cares for me each and every day. I look around me, and I see so many lives that are not rewarded with a life like mine. It pains my heart to see a person or a child not given an opportunity to be like me with a pure body and mind, a family, and a home. I was spared from a life of disadvantage and hardship and was given the chance to live a life with love and without pain.

Uncertain Future

In your lifetime, you may be experiencing a deep depression, leaving you torn between your family and the desire to move on with your life so that you can have the change that is desperately needed. You want the best of both worlds, but know in your heart that you must choose between giving up what you worked so hard to achieve and beginning a new but uncertain future. When encountering such a dilemma, you must reach deep down in your soul to evaluate your situation and to realize that your decision will affect your physical and emotional well-being. If you continue on a course of confusion and indecision, your psychological state will be unbalanced, and your entire family structure will be placed in jeopardy if you fail to make the wise choice.

Losing Hope

If you lose hope, there is no escape. The only way out is from within. Your life is worth living, so find the strength to free yourself from the past and to know that there is hope in the future.

Never Give Up

Understanding your future is very important and critical in your quest for success and happiness. If you focus on your future goals and ambitions, you will overcome obstacles and barriers that the world places in your way. These obstructions are little more than temporary setbacks on your journey in life. Always be aware and conscious of your insight and vision, never giving up on your goals and aspirations.

My Life Of Lonliness

Days go by, and nothing changes for me. I am alone and without a companion to call my own. This is such an empty feeling, and I find myself in total despair, unable to see an end to my loneliness. It is hard for any person to feel this way when isolation is an everyday experience. At times I want to give up and accept my life of loneliness. The only hope I have is to believe in myself and to wait for the day when this feeling will no longer be part of my life.

The Well of Life

When I gaze deep down into the well, darkness and emptiness are within. I think back to a time when there was no way to escape the well. As I struggled to free myself from within, I slipped further away from the light and became lost and afraid. Faith and courage were all I had left, or my life would remain forever within the empty well.

Fear And Resentment

What can a controlling nature do in your relationship? It creates fear, hatred, and hostility. More importantly, it degrades the victim of manipulation to a state of emotional damage. He or she withdraws, putting distance between the couple. Do not allow yourself to be in a controlling relationship. Do not be a victim of its negativity and guilt. It is important to use rejection as a learning tool to improve self-respect and dignity. Transform rejection into a positive mental viewpoint.

Facing Reality

When life's difficult moments challenge you, you must rise to the occasion and confront reality. The dilemmas you face present you with moments to reflect upon your life and what you have accomplished. You are at a crucial stage, and you must allow your mind to take control to focus on your true identity and future aspirations. In the end, you will be a better person for yourself and others once you accept the truth and have a vision that will allow you to live a life free of fear, anxiety, and pain.

The Future Is Now

Your life is like a ticking clock, and whether you realize it or not,your hopes and dreams are passing you by. It is up to you to find a new way tounderstand yourself. You must live in the present and not in the past. The future is now.

Control Your Thoughts

The mind can play a major role in accepting what has been a gift to you at the inception of your life. Who you are and what you are will determine your happiness and fulfillment as a person. It is important to recognize the less fortunate around you and realize what has been given to you will never cause you envy, shame, or resentment of others. You will be a person who lived a life never having feelings about others who have had more success, advantages, and possessions. Remember, envy can destroy your mind if you allow it to control your thoughts and mentality.

Overcoming Hardship

I have to believe in myself, and I have to have integrity. It is my destiny, and now I know right from wrong and the consequences of my actions. That was the magical hand that helped me find my real self. It was a stepping stone in my life that put me back on the right path. I want to make my family and the people who care about me proud of me.

Imaginary Vision

In my thoughts, I sense harmony, peacefulness, and tranquility embrace my spirit. My world is eternal, uncertain, and insecure. My expectations color my existence, and my imagined vision becomes a symbol of beauty. Truth and insufferable tragedies stem from my search to find a perfect world. Awakening from my sleep, I imagine a new dawn. In the end, my fictitious world fades from my view.

All Over Again

If I had to do it all over again, what would my life be like today? In my mind, if I had followed my heart, would that have made a difference? I have made many mistakes because I now know I am not perfect. I have come a long way and have learned to accept my fate. The many rejections that I have endured have caused me pain and anguish, and I nearly lost my way. I was given a second chance, unlike others who were not granted that opportunity, and with my strength and determination, I was blessed to live my life all over again.

Determination

Determination means having the positive attitude of never giving up and always finding ways to achieve success and happiness. It requires that you stay focused on your goals and not have outside influences distract you from gaining your desired objective. Determination is a mental force, and it is up to you to take advantage of this ability by stimulating your mind to rise above the material barriers that are negative forces interfering with your progress in life.

Your True Feelings

Feelings show what kind of person you will develop into as life goes on. There comes a time in your life when you will face uncertain emotional changes that will cause you anxiety and depression. The strength within you will allow you to understand the hurt and sorrow you or your loved ones are suffering. Don't be afraid to show your true feelings, which will help you become a warm and sincere person for yourself and others.

Optimism And Hope

Having a positive attitude and a belief that situations will be resolved favorably can lead to your having a positive influence on the world. An optimist is any individual who has taken a positive view of his or her life and accepts that the most suitable outcome will occur. When you apply optimism to your strategy and goals in life, you will achieve only success, and this will cause your state of mind to alter and improve your outlook in life. Hope is a special feeling in your heart. It creates a desire that what you wish for can be achieved. Hope makes you feel confidence in yourself and the world around you. It allows you to strive for happiness, to bring pleasure to your soul, and to believe that whatever you hope for within time will be yours forever.

The Loss of Innocence

You woke up like an angel that morning, full of happiness and love in your heart. When you smiled, it was a delight for all to see. Your time spent with us was like heaven on earth. We all ask ourselves why you were taken from us so quickly and without any good explanation. Maybe, in time, we will understand why. It broke our hearts to lose you, but you did not go alone because part of us went with you on that sad day. We will always remember you, and the music you loved will play on forever to remind us of you.

Happiness

Happiness is a physical and emotional feeling of contentment and satisfaction. It is a deep appreciation and knowledge that fills your heart and mind with peace and tranquility. It is an unbelievable sensation in your inner self. When there is little hope for finding happiness, such a feeling will cause you to feel differently about yourself and your surroundings. When you are in need of love and are suffering from financial need, you will find happiness when someone reaches out to you and provides that pleasure.

Pressures and Burdens In Our Lives

With each day, into our lives come new pressures and burdens, which we must confront and challenge. We must take the time to reflect upon past mistakes and discover our true feelings and real desires. Our enlightened with our lives will create a clearer vision as we encounter emotional confusion and difficulty. When we reach this point, we will be able to foresee our lives in our own way and not allow suppressive forces to burden us and prevent us from attaining our future goals and potential.

Walking Alone

When I woke up I found myself on a dark, narrow path leading nowhere. There was nothing in my life but confusion and hopelessness. With no one to help me, I felt like I was walking alone without any direction. As I took several steps forward, I saw many choices before me, and that gave me a reason to move on with my life. At first I was fearful of the unknown and what it would do to me. I needed to find closure before it was too late. I had to find myself and discover who I really am and where I am going. My state of mind was unstable, and I feared the worst when I was alone with my thoughts and feelings. Now I realize there is a reason to go on with my life and to be happy again. I have found what I have been looking for, and it is you.

Survival

He wasn't going to be outgunned. He kept his eye on the ball at all times. That was his life to reach his goal. In his heart, he knew he was right; he could do no wrong. He had to fight, and if this meant constant maneuverings, so be it. Even though the toll that this took was devastating to him, he never gave up. In the end, he triumphed over evil.

Emotional Control

What makes us lose emotional control and cause hurt and pain in others? Sometimes we are weak and have a low tolerance for disagreement. If this feeling persists, it can have dire consequences, causing unnecessary upset and bitterness. This friction can be healed by taking a time-out and stepping back from antagonism and hostility. Developing the ability to do so takes time, but once you recognize it, you will be able to adapt and increase your emotional control.

Power Of The Mind

Power of the mind is an awesome and unbelievable feeling that can propel you to accomplish and accelerate the achievement of your goals. It is vital to appreciate that it controls your journey along the path of life, helping you to obtain happiness and pleasure. It is important for every individual to use the mind to its fullest capacity and not be controlled by and fear. If you take care of your body, your mind will be protected from losing all you have attained in your life. Your mind and spirit are within you for all eternity, and you must use your power of mind to do good for yourself and others.

What Has Happened To Us?

Although we have had a beautiful family and wonderful memories that will always persist, we can no longer continue because my life has changed, and, unfortunately, we have grown apart. I must be honest with you; this new relationship I have experienced makes it impossible for me to continue our friendship. Please try to understand so you will realize what has happened in our lives. In my mind you will always be a dear and special person, and I will cherish the past we had together. I pray that one day our paths will cross again and our family and friendship will be restored.

Words of Love

If we keep words deep inside, they remain a hollow symbol of love. Words can never fully capture the powerful emotions within our hearts and souls. Communicate your feelings and experience the love. Your life is a journey from the past to your future. Search deep for negative influences and replace them with positive energy. Understand the strength within your soul and make each day bring you closer to your true feelings.

Knowing Yourself

What can I offer to my world that I am thankful to be part of?
I must first look into myself to understand and appreciate the
beauty that was given to me. It has taken time for me to grow and
to understand how important it is for me to truly love myself. This
feeling of love allows me to love others and to feel their pain and
suffering. If you cannot find love in your heart and soul, loneliness
and frustration will overcome your chances to love yourself and
know who you
really are.

Desires of Love

I reflect upon my love life and accept that the feelings I encounter
will create intense desires, emotional fulfillment, and happiness
blessed with passionate love. There will be times of disappointment
and sorrow in my soul. I fear that all hope will be lost, and love will be
a distant memory. I know there will be many nights when I am awake
thinking about what I would have done differently. I would still be in
love today. In time, with faith and courage, I can overcome my pain
and suffering so I can love again

From the Heart

I could be wrong in my mind, but when I view the universe
through my heart, I feel close to what I am searching for. There is so
much doubt and confusion in my mind that I must allow my heart
to guide me through the chaos and make positive choices for my
life. Only through my heart will I find the true happiness I have been
unable to feel for so long. In the end, I must trust what's in my heart
and believe in myself.

Don't Be Discouraged

In times of confusion and uncertainty, don't be discouraged.

When you are down on your luck, don't be discouraged.

When the love of your life disappoints you, don't be discouraged.

When your friends abandon you, don't be discouraged.

Trust yourself and be yourself, and you will not be discouraged..

Now I Realize

Imagine the time when your true love no longer loves and cares for you. That pain in your heart will live forever, and the close relationship you once had will never come back. Your life will forever change because the feelings you once had are gone. That hardship within yourself will overwhelm you identity. You will question and blame yourself, thinking that you should have done more to protect your relationship that was once so strong and beautiful. Will she forgive me for not understanding her wants and needs? I will suffer mentally and spiritually each day we are apart and you are no longer in my life. I wait by my phone to hear your voice, but you never call, and now I realize how much I have lost because I do not have you. Now I must move on and start a new life without you.

Deep Within Your Heart

All the simple things in life can be achieved and bring happiness to your soul. But you have to imagine a vision of love before you can experience that happiness. So much time and energy is spent on improving our status in life that we lose sight of what's really important. Your life's journey will succeed when you realize the true meaning that lies deep within your heart.

e.

Change Is Good

There comes a time in our lives when we must make a change before it is too late and you regret what your life has become and what you have failed to accomplish. You have to look at your life and use your feelings to guide you and to show you the way.

Do not fear change. Hold onto to the good, remove the negative in your life and recreate yourself in a new image. This will take time, courage and determination. Be strong, stay focused and never let your dreams fade away.

Time Is On My Side

I look around and see so many lives that have meaning and purpose. Many years have gone by and I feel hopeless and in despair. I find it difficult with little opportunity in sight to feel positive about my life and future. The days feel like years, but I know that time is on my side and I must refuse to give up in my quest for happiness and success.

IV

Social
Behavior

Breaking The Bond

When families fail and the many years of nurturing and bonding are challenged, the child will have to accept a new identity in order to overcome this hardship and turmoil for which he or she is not   responsible. When love and affection are no longer felt, the consequences will be life changing, unpredictable, and deeply confusing for any young, vulnerable child. The stability that was once created is now missing, and the child is left to drift into a path of uncertainty. It is crucial that we pause and reflect upon the damage that we will cause by removing the structure and support system that a healthy and intact family provides to children. We owe it to our children to always remember that their lives and happiness must be safeguarded and protected no matter how difficult the family circumstances may be.

Children Of The World

The number one concern in our world is protecting our children from dangerous influences that are a constant threat to their innocence and happiness. They are so precious and vulnerable. So many children have either suffered or died in vain because they never had the opportunity to express their true feelings and to live a normal life as a child. It is the responsibility of our society to be the guardians and role models for the children of the world. We must never forget the children who were not given the chance to blossom and share in the life of all the other children who were blessed with love and compassion.

Consider The Consequences

It is important to understand, as an adolescent youth, the elements of society in order to prepare for your future success in life. You will one day come to a crossroad where you will have to decide what direction you will take, and this will determine your longevity and happiness. You will encounter endless temptations that will threaten your survival and contentment and involve you in crime, drugs, and a life of hardship. It is critical to understand that it takes only one error to change the course of your life, so always consider the consequences of your actions before you fulfill your deepest desires.

Quality Of Existence

Society and the factors that contribute to the downfall of both young and old individuals are influencing the manner in which we live. The factors include the criminal element that encompasses all segments of life. What we observe and listen to affects the quality of our existence and will ultimately erase the gains that took so long for us to accomplish. With hard work and perseverance, we can eliminate the toxic environment that has caused instability in our society.

Never Give Up And Always Remember

We come into this world knowing that good and evil are forces in the world that will confront us as we live our lives. We must distinguish between them. Each one of us has the will and desire to spread love and not destruction and hate. If we can overcome the many differences among us, then we can begin to see and hope for peace and harmony. The many lives that have been sacrificed for good must always be remembered for their patriotism in preserving our freedom and way of life.

Problems Caused By Society

Your mind, your body, and your self-esteem are greatly affected when you are repeatedly rejected, and your emotional stability is torn and tormented through no fault of your own. A loss of hope will overpower you when there is no opportunity or reason to believe in yourself so you can overcome your despair and regain your dignity. Your feelings will play a major role in what can be detrimental to your success and happiness in life. You must guard against the weakness in yourself, which will determine your faith and ability to fight the evil spirit that controls your mind and body. Always remember that it is not your fault, and you must never blame yourself for the problems caused by society.

How Precious Is Life

When entering this world of ours, we envision long, healthy, and beautiful lives. Sadly, many of us will never experience the joys and fulfillment that life provides for us. We must recognize that we live in a world with much uncertainty, sickness, and violence. Life is random, and fate plays a major role; we are powerless in controlling what may afflict us as we go through life. It is frightening to confront this reality, and we must be diligent and emotionally strong to withstand and survive what lies ahead because life is so precious.

Your Life

Your future belongs to you. Go forward with passion in your heart, and that will bring you success and happiness. Your limitations must not hold you back from your own happiness. It lies within your soul to express what you really feel. Life has many dimensions, and you must explore them all to find out who you really are and who you could be, so never stop searching for the truth.

A Decaying Society

What we are witnessing in our world today is a decline in the moral and social fabric of our civilization. This current state of affairs is damaged and afflicted by our neglect and failure to accept responsibility to protect and defend our living conditions and quality of life experiences. As a civilized society, we must never compromise our freedoms and way of life. We must take all steps necessary to preserve our existence and survival as a human race. If we do not confront this serious alteration, we will be faced ultimately with a progressive and chilling demise that will set us back for years to come. We must provide guidance and values to bring about effective alternatives in order to bring about a more stable, secure, and productive lifestyle.

We Must Teach

We must teach our youth so that they understand the importance of education and the role it plays in their lives. Strong family values must be stressed so that children know that they have opportunities for employment with the help of a strong, intact family unit. I want to stress in no uncertain terms that all of our children must receive quality education so that we as a society will be able to prepare and continue to be the beacon of educational opportunities throughout the world.

Family Values

Family values are vital to an efficient and well-functioning society. They provide the foundation and the basis for constructive and meaningful growth in both the individual and the family. These values include a deep faith in God and respect for oneself and for other human beings, especially for our children and all those who live in our world. Only when these values are accepted and adopted by all of our society can we achieve a nonviolent world where we can live in peace and harmony together.

Weakening Of Family

Since the weakening of family values, our society has lost a decade of our youth to crime, drug use, underage drinking, teenage pregnancy, and premature death. Besides the horrific decline in our young generation, we must never forget the many victims who have survived serious violent acts only to live a sad life of hardship, pain, and suffering. One can only imagine the anguish a parent experiences knowing that his or her child will live a life in a wheelchair because our society allowed the disintegration of the family unit and family values. All of these toxic results can be reversed by a return to morality and stability provided by the family and the institutions of our society. Only when we focus on family in our society will we begin to change the mental dependency that has deprived us and our children of a happy and secure family life.

Improve Within Ourselves

Like all cultures that exist in the United States and throughout the world, we must improve within ourselves and build upon all of the successes that we have been so fortunate to experience. Only through education will one truly pursue life's dreams and increase one's livelihood and financial capacity. Education in our society must be equal for all groups regardless of ethnicity or background. It must be available for every individual so that no one is left behind and without the hope of a fulfilling future, a secure job, and a family to support.

Cycles Of Life

It is very true that history repeats itself in everyone's life. Life is a precious gift given to us from above, and we must defend, protect, and preserve it at all costs. The loss of any life is a travesty and confusing to the human mind. The cycles of life continue to influence our behavior and the way we experience happiness, sadness, success, and failure. As humans, we adapt to our surroundings and learn to accept what transpires over our lifetime.

Respect

In life, you first have to respect yourself. Only then can you respect others, including friends, family, and loved ones. When you give respect to those you meet, you will experience in return a sense of satisfaction and comfort knowing that you created permanent bonds of loyalty with them. If we all respect one another, the world will be a better place. This respect will dictate a mutual understanding no matter your race or ethnic background.

Divided Family

The moral decay in our society is a contributing factor in the continued weakening and deterioration of the family structure in our world and throughout social relationships. The separation and division of parents due to alienation and emotional instability have jeopardized our youth and have caused a decline in educational growth, psychological development, and the opportunity to enjoy a mature intact biological family. The final obstacle that has afflicted our nuclear family and that has made it more difficult for relationships to survive is the loss of dignity and sanity between a man and a woman in a romantic commitment in our society today. We must return to and encourage the traditional values that support love and harmony, and we must learn how to preserve a lasting and sacred trust in one another and social understanding.

Family Disintegration

We must do everything in our power as guardians to protect the innocent minds and hearts of our children in order for them to thrive and prosper. We must provide the foundation to allow children to experience stable, loving, and moral direction so that they can understand and appreciate the meaning of life. It has taken several decades to undermine the role of the family and cause serious social behavior in our youth and adolescents. This disintegration has also caused a decline in every area of life and an increase in crime, poverty, and emotional crises among our youth.

Intimidation

Intimidation can be extremely devastating to your mental and physical well-being. It can be an obstacle to your character and personal growth potential. It must be challenged strenuously so that fear does not conquer hope in reaching your future goals. To defeat intimidation, you must take active steps to eliminate the threat. This will give you a second chance to live a life free from guilt and pain. It takes an understanding that if you have jealousy in your heart, it will place distance between you and your partner and cause your relationship to become controlling and distrustful.

Peer Pressure

Peer pressure comes from the feeling of wanting to be accepted and have equality with our friends and associates. Only you can choose between positive and negative peer pressure. It is important to choose wisely because this will determine your future success. Peer pressure can overwhelm any individual and can lead to destruction, crime, drug abuse, and gang-related activities.

Temptation

In life, as we grow we develop and are cultivated for good by our parents and society. During your life's journey, it is important to do good for yourself and others. There will be times in your life when you will be persuaded to choose that which is regarded as unwise or wrong. Resist and overcome the pressure of temptation. Your mind and spirit play a major role in eliminating and avoiding temptation. Once you cross over and sin, your soul becomes immune and loses its free will to choose what is good. To overcome temptation, you must consider the consequences of your actions, realizing the danger that you are causing to yourself and others.

Influencing

Society and the cause that contribute to the downfall of both young and old are influencing our behavior. The factors include the criminal element that includes all segments of life. What we observe and listen to affects the quality of our existence and will ultimately erase the gains that took so long to accomplish. These severe changes in our lives have dramatically changed the way we live, and only time and hard work can provide a happier life.

Problems Caused By Society

Your mind, your body, and your self-esteem are greatly affected when you are repeatedly rejected, and your emotional stability is torn and tormented through no fault of your own. A loss of hope will overpower you when there is no opportunity or reason to believe in yourself so you can overcome your despair and regain your dignity. Your feelings will play a major role in what can be detrimental to your success and happiness in life. You must guard against the weakness in yourself, which will determine your faith and ability to fight the evil spirit that controls your mind and body. Always remember that it is not your fault, and you must never blame yourself for the problems caused by society.

Educational and Criminal Sub-Culture

Of ultimate concern is addressing the criminal subculture and addressing the issues that need to be inculcated in our children to show them the dangers of crime and the harmful effects that drugs and a lack of education produce. For without the strong foundation of education, there will be less opportunity for the creation of resources, which will lead to frustration, desperation, and criminal wrongdoing.

Ability To Survive

It is not enough to play soccer and to have strong family values. What is necessary is the ability to survive. Young people are often led astray by the dominant culture, only to discover ruin and destruction and sometimes death. The fact remains that it is the environment that cannot be controlled and that causes any decent individual to stumble and to become overwhelmed by the forces pivoted against him or her.

Endless Hardship

The amount of greed that has existed throughout history is outrageous. If we continue along this path, our existence and quality of life will be in jeopardy, and a serious decline in human living conditions will be beyond our ability to alter. The ability of most of us to survive and lead a normal, productive, and rewarding life will be beyond our grasp. Without the satisfaction of being afforded the basic comforts of life, we will have no alternative but to accept a life of starvation, disease, deprivation, and criminal activity, to live day to day through a vicious cycle of endless hardship.

I Have Seen It All

I have seen it all, and I have witnessed many a friend and relative fail because of the lack of insight and common sense. I do not wish to preach to the world, but I am compelled to state the following: If you neglect your education and you give more time to drinking, using drugs, and surrounding yourself with negative role models, you are headed down a road of missed opportunities, regrets, and misfortune. Failure is easy to attain, and I do not want anyone to go down a road where there is nothing but a dead end street.

Failure

Believe it can happen and it will. Failure is only in your mind, and you must overcome it. Without confidence in yourself, you will spiral down into loneliness, depression, and despair. Avoid this state at all costs or you will become lost and confused, and it will be difficult to find your way home. Always have a positive viewpoint and think before you act. During these bad economic times, it is easy to become depressed and sad for unknown reasons. This feeling grows not from the outside world but from within yourself. Only you have the power to alter that feeling.

Common Sense

What does it take to have common sense? Common sense is a gift that you are born with, and it cannot be taught in school or learned through experience. Every decision made with common sense is a wise and significant choice. It is based on sound reasoning and cannot be challenged.

Beauty of Life

No matter how much evil is in the world, we must always remember the beauty of life. One day in the future, with dedication and determination, we can live in a world where we have eliminated poverty, disease, and horrific crimes against humanity. The people who suffer the most are the young and vulnerable, whom we must protect at all costs for them to survive and for whom we must have hope that they will not die in vain, that their lives have meaning in the world. This can only happen when we declare that humanity will put an end to its inhumanity and selfishness. Only this can save the less fortunate among us and bring about a better world for all.

Hatred

People have been affected by hatred since the beginning of mankind. It has taken millions of lives and has caused untold pain and suffering. You will always experience hatred because it is man-made and is a control mechanism. When you are overcome by hatred and anger, your mind can no longer function rationally, and you are driven by a deep desire to act out your psychological defects. Hatred is a powerful and damaging emotional trait that has caused untold wars, violence, and mistrust, as well as fear and terror in man's heart. Only when we begin to realize the destructive nature of hatred and the devastating impact it has had on the human race can we then challenge the forces of hatred and evil in our world and create an atmosphere of love, peace, and understanding. Man's mission is to study and find meaningful paths to work vigorously to understand all the past violence, bloodshed, and genocidal consequences that have eliminated portions of the human race.

Survivors

Since the beginning of time, man has suffered through all kinds of trauma, sickness, and diseases that have caused death, pain, and suffering as well as psychological and emotional scars. Human history will reveal how over time we have progressed to become a modern industrialized world that has produced both positive and negative outcomes for the human condition. Science has yet to discover the underlying causes of unexplainable and irreversible sicknesses and diseases. We have come a long way in our efforts to eradicate the many illnesses and disorders of both the body and mind. Our immune systems are incapable of the harsh realities that force us to succumb to industrialized, man-made diseases.

Pride

Having pride is not a negative. It is a feeling of accomplishment inside yourself that raises your sense of dignity, merit, and importance. In order to experience pride, you must first recognize your own self-esteem, which is an important part of your upbringing and good character. This trait of pride can be fostered, encouraged, and developed by giving credit to those we love and wish to see succeed.

Have We Gone Wrong?

When the world was formed, it was a beautiful, peaceful, and pristine landscape. It was a time of extraordinary creation in harmony with all creatures given to support the universe. This period in history was a time when there was balance and coexistence in the kingdoms that lasted eons. Our diversified planet, which is blessed with an abundance of natural resources, is in a decline toward corruption and decay. It was human greed that became the focus of man's accomplishments without regard to the damage and consequences   during his development, which continues to this day. This philosophical approach through history has contributed to the decrease in great amounts of life for centuries.

Cycles of Life

It is very true that history repeats itself in everyone's life. Life is a precious gift given to us from above, and we must defend, protect, and preserve it at all costs. The loss of any life is a travesty and confusing to the human mind. The cycles of life continue to influence our behavior and the way we experience happiness, sadness, success, and failure. As humans, we adapt to our surroundings and learn to accept what transpires over our lifetime.

Manners

You always start out in life with a positive viewpoint toward others, showing them politeness, respect, and kindness. There is no reason to treat someone with discourtesy even when that person shows you little regard and few manners. It is important to adopt manners beginning at a very young age. This will enable you to interact affirmatively, which reflects on your reputation and character. Using good manners in your everyday affairs will have a lasting impact on society and reduce hostility, tension, and disagreements.

Freedom

Countless lives have been lost fighting for individual freedom and a life of peace, harmony, and tranquility. Unfortunately, many have not had the privilege to experience the freedoms that we enjoy as Americans each and every day. We take our freedoms for granted and fail to consider and appreciate the many victims who have suffered and died at the hands of dysfunctional countries that suppress and deny a life of freedom without fear of slavery, suffering, and genocide. It is difficult to envision the torment and uncertainty that people feel knowing that freedom is stripped from all aspects of life without the possibility or opportunity to have their mind in full control of their life and destiny. For thousands of years, we have seen mankind enslaved by ruthless and powerful evil forces and people whose main goal is to control and dictate the conditions that make us free. We must never succumb to these forces, and we must work to cure and protect the many who have struggled to secure and maintain their freedom. It is important that we never forget all those without a chance to enjoy their precious life to fulfillment. We must strive to continue to protect and defend all who desire the values of life, liberty, and freedom.

Fighting the Odds

Growing up in today's world can be challenging and confusing to the young and vulnerable mind. The temptation that surrounds each and every one of us can cause serious, permanent psychological and physical consequences. From an early age, all types of abuse confront our young people, and many of them will succumb to the glorification of a subculture that seeks to control the minds and lifestyles of those who are innocent and vulnerable. The responsible segments of our society must teach and promote strong values so the young can distinguish right from wrong and know they can succeed, both now and in the future. We have lost too many children to bullying and abuse, and we must never accept or tolerate the agony and destruction of prolonged manipulation and intimidation. This writing should make you aware of the many young boys and girls who either took their own lives or were victims of domestic violence and murder. As you move forward with the gift of life, always remember the consequences of your actions before you make important decisions so you will live a life filled with hope, prosperity,

Problems Caused By Society

Your mind, your body, and your self-esteem are greatly affected when you are repeatedly rejected, and your emotional stability is torn and tormented through no fault of your own. A loss of hope will overpower you when there is no opportunity or reason to believe in yourself so you can overcome your despair and regain your dignity. Your feelings will play a major role in what can be detrimental to your success and happiness in life. You must guard against the weakness in yourself, which will determine your faith and ability to fight the evil spirit that controls your mind and body. Always remember that it is not your fault, and you must never blame yourself for the problems caused by society.

Lost At Sea

The ocean is a cosmic world of both life and death. There are stories to be told of great accomplishments and tragedies that engulf our curiosity and temptation. The forces of nature control man's destiny, hopes, and needs. All life arose from the sea, which is also the most powerful creator of death. Our oceans must not be taken for granted but must be respected by all. It is a difficult scenario when the oceans reclaim a life without explanation and understanding. The treacherous seas have swept up thousands of lives since the beginning of time. We have suffered a great deal at the hands of the seas and will never cease to do so. We can only hope that our oceans and seas give us a reason why there are so many loved ones who become victims of the great phenomenon that controls our world and our future.

Our Values

We have come to the point in time where we have lost sight of the true values that unite and promote our common heritage to love, honor, and cherish life and the pursuit of happiness. Without strong values, it would be impossible for our society to overcome detrimental forces that challenge our existence and our way of life. If we count the senseless lives that have been taken over hundreds of years, so many families have been impacted and destroyed. Because of man's inhumanity to man and lack of respect for one another, many lives have been taken that could have been with us today.

One Error In Judgement

In life's difficult moments, your survival is always at risk. Beware and protect yourself from external threats from any source. Life is so tenuous that one error in judgment can cost everything you have worked for.

Departure From Us

It is one of the greatest feelings of man to be able to experience the ability to fly at will. We were gifted with the opportunity and the knowledge to propel ourselves into the heavens. Just as our oceans and seas challenged us to explore her depths, we now have the ingenuity to conquer our atmosphere and beyond. We must appreciate and understand the consequences when we ascend and discover our skies and universe. Today we have the luxury of being able to travel to all destinations of our world, but this comes with a great risk when we take the chance to explore and adventure in the air. We must never forget the many thousands who have perished above and across the universe. These sudden losses of life are more tragic when we understand that in using this ability to fly, we will experience many casualties and tragedies in the air. It is painful to bear the loss of precious lives knowing they will never come home again. We can only imagine in our hearts the fear and agony before they left our world. Their spirits will live on forever, and they will never be forgotten.

Selfishness

When you place your self-interest before that of others, you display a narrow-minded and one-dimensional image. You believe that the world revolves around your needs and wants and that no one else matters. You appear to be interesting but never interested in the world around you. Selfishness creates a distance between you and those you love and causes distrust, resentment, and isolation.

What We Desire

The mind plays a different role for men and women, and we have to understand and respect how we interact with another. The desire we possess shapes the way we have looked at the world and other human beings since the beginning of time. When our creator molded the female mind, it was made to appreciate beauty and compassion within their hearts and souls. This foundation depends on stability, growth, and long-lasting love. With these traits, all families will be granted happy and secure lives. A woman pursues her hopes and dreams for the future and focuses on raising a family. Her hope is to keep the family safe and free from evil influences from the outside world.

Living In A Make-believe World

It is shameful that we allow so much disease-infected poverty, starvation, and unnecessary death in a world where there is so much wealth, prosperity, and apparent happiness. Yet we ignore the harsh reality, pain, and suffering that surrounds us each and every day.

Envision the children literally starving to death because they have nothing to eat and no medical treatment to bring them back to life. How would you live with yourself as a parent with the knowledge that our baby would experience a world without food, medicine, or an opportunity to live a better life? It is sad that the world fails to recognize hundreds of years of starvation and is still unable to solve this unacceptable and forbidden tragedy.

We live in a society where governments and people make millions of dollars while children starve to death, children who are so tender and precious and could belong to you. God is looking down upon our world and is ashamed at what we have become by failing to provide the essential conditions for survival.

V

Prayers

Mother And Child

As a mother, I believe that all of my children are equally loved. One day, an angel appeared in my life and brought you to me. As time went by, you developed into a sweet child and loving person, an inspiration to me. You fulfilled all my hopes and dreams when you came into my world, and you made my life a joy and comfort in having you. I know in time you will move on in our precious life, and as a mother, I will have to suffer not being with you. May you be blessed and preserved, and may God keep you all the days of your life. I am thankful for having lived my life with you. I pray to the heavens that the Lord protects you and provides you with His gentle love and mercy. My life has been fulfilled knowing you have been a

It Is Up To The Lord

It is up to the Lord and yourself to decide where your life will take you. We do not know what the future holds for us. Some of us will be blessed with certain qualities of life and be granted a better chance to survive. But there are many of us who will not be afforded a full and productive life. In your heart, you must understand the suffering of others and pray to the Lord to give them a new beginning in life and erase all of the hardship they have been through.

A Child in Need

Every child should have a family that provides love, care, and a stable home. Many children do not have access to a feeling of love and a sense of belonging to a family. Those children are so sensitive and vulnerable that society must do everything possible to ensure their well-being so they can achieve the growth they deserve.

A Prayer Of Hope

When you find yourself in times of trouble and at the lowest level of survival, there is only one vision that will save you and raise you beyond despair. Have a deep belief in your heart that faith will prevail and that you will conquer your fears. Do not give up on yourself, and give hope a chance to flourish within you. This feeling of devotion and belief will empower you to accomplish your goals and achieve success in all your deeds.

Our Innocent Ones

When I look up to the Heavens, seeking answers to why our innocent children are made to suffer and die, it makes my heart break. They were never given the opportunity to enjoy life and all its pleasures, to smile, laugh, cry, play, and grow in loving, nurturing families. Each time an innocent child is taken from us, a part of me dies as well. I continue to look for answers to why they leave us so young, but I can find none. I can only hope and pray that the Lord works harder to protect and defend all our little angels and keep them from pain.

Which Way To Turn

After the loss of a loved one, you will find yourself in a state of fear and emotional weakness. There will be many dark days when you are alone and ask yourself, "Why couldn't the Lord take me?" Days will go by and you will find yourself lost and confused, not knowing which way to turn. You will become possessed by past feelings and memories. All you can do at this time is to believe in yourself, knowing that with the Lord's help, you will be able to understand why you had to bear a sacrificial hardship in your life.

What Do Children Need?

All children deserve a future that will bring them success and happiness. Without love and protection, children have no chance to survive and thrive in the world in which we live today. These innocent and vulnerable children require a deep and lasting commitment to ensure that their well-being both physically and emotionally is safeguarded from the world we live in.

When children are neglected and abused, our hearts cry out with pain and sorrow. We must all be aware of what they are going through and the fear that they are witnessing. We must do everything in our power to ease their suffering and to protect all children from further harm so that they can experience the pleasures of life and achieve success and happiness.

A Victim's Prayer

You cannot imagine the feeling that comes over you when you first experience the loss of your only child. This emotional grief will overwhelm you and tear your life apart as you sink deeper into denial, anger, and panic. You refuse to accept the truth and confront this horrible reality that your child is no longer alive and part of your world. As days go by, your mind keeps falling deeper into a state of depression as you struggle to overcome the loss, and you still find imprisoned by emotional pain. You will find the strength to your loss and why your life was changed by the Lord. you see the light and begin to feel that the Lord will cept your new life, and one day you will be with your child again for all eternity.

Loss Of A Child

In life, we strive to create a family to enable us to show love and bring joy for the children who are gifts to us from the Lord. We must never cease to pray for all those families who were once blessed with a child and thought they had everything in life. We must always remember the pain and anguish when a parent experiences the loss of their only child and is not granted the gift to have another. We must continue to pray for their loss and to have trust in God to ease their trauma and burden. As humans, we fail to appreciate what has happened to such a family and that this fate could happen to us. Pray to the heavens and ask the Lord to protect and spare you from such a tragedy.

A Chrismas Poem

During the Christmas season, we must pause and reflect upon our faith in God, asking for peace and justice for all mankind. The violence, destruction, and despair witnessed throughout the world over thousands of years must be replaced with compassion and understanding, which can be granted only with the help of God's divine grace. We must continue to strive and work hard to eliminate hatred, injustice, and deadly violence against the Lord's children.

Sense Of Hope

Pray for our deceased with humble and contrite hea
hope and forgiveness. We pray for past and present
torment our souls. Knowing that life will never be the
forward with a deep sense of not knowing the cause
pray for strength, courage, and vision that the futur
pain and suffering and bring new light and a ne

What Other's Don't Have

There are many of us who do not have the happiness that can be awarded in life. My heart breaks when I think of all those who were never given the chance to experience the love of their own. Always remember the emotional suffering a man and woman endure because they weren't afforded the opportunity to fall in love and have what other families were given from the Lord. Honor what you have, and show compassion for the less fortunate ones among us.

A Parent's Pain

Only a parent can understand the agony and pain felt when a child is afflicted with disease or has never been given the opportunity to live a full and happy life. The child's anguish is difficult to accept, and as a parent, we have to provide strength, hope, and courage to overcome the fear and confusion that the child is experiencing. We must always keep faith alive, pray for recovery, and never forget the many innocent children who gave up their lives believing that God would reward them with a special life with Him in heaven.

They Were Not Responsible

For all the precious children around the world suffering from starvation and sickness through no fault of their own, we must never forget their plight in not having the opportunity to enjoy and experience a full childhood. And to the victims of natural disasters and accidents, we always remember their fate of death for which they were not responsible. We ask that you continue to bless and protect all your children wherever they may be and unite all of us in a world where there is calm, love, and harmony.

Let Us Strive

Let us strive to understand each other more deeply and to commit to one another in a full expression of support so that there will be mutual love, respect, and understanding for each another's needs, wishes, and desires. For this reason, it is essential for all families to appreciate this God-given teaching so that animosity can be extinguished in our lives. Families will be able to endure dysfunctional upset and stress, which will enable all families to prosper and exhibit true love.

A Petition To The Lord

Dear Lord, we wish to be close to you and to know you during our lives, and we offer our prayer to you for all those whom we have lost since the beginning of time when you created us in your image. We ask you, Lord, why is there so much war, sickness, and disease in our world? So, dear Lord, we ask that you receive our prayers and always remember those who sacrificed there lives in wars; victims of crime, including those unfortunate ones who were murdered or battered or who had their lives violently taken from them; loved ones who suffered through sickness and disease; and parents who endured the unnecessary and tragic death of their own children.

Moment To Reflect

God made women who were chosen to be special in life. The love and passion within a woman will be a source of strength and joy for the entire world. The angels sent you upon me with your tender touch and smile. I was blessed when you became a part of my life to share your love with me. There are many beautiful women who were granted a full life of being loved and showing love. But we must always keep in our prayers all those precious women whose lives were viciously taken through no fault of their own. When you read this prayer, take a moment to reflect upon the sudden loss of a woman who should have lived a long and beautiful life. We can only pray that she will find peace in a new world of nonviolence.

Healing Miracles

There are many miracles of healing from uncertainty. With faith, belief, and support, you will overcome this difficult time. Try to understand why you were chosen for this kind of ending. All you want is one more chance to keep your precious life that was given to you. As difficult as it may be, we both know in our hearts that the Lord made the right decision, and in time we can triumph over this terrifying illness.

Believe in Who You Are

You have been given a body and soul from birth, and you must always protect, preserve, and cherish yourself. Your life can be a fulfillment of all your hopes and dreams only if you truly believe in who you are. Once you accept yourself, you will be able to love what has been given to you as a gift from the heavens.

Conquering Hope

There are some of us in this world who are chosen to endure the misfortunes of life and to experience the pain and suffering of body and mind. Mankind has come a long way in conquering and eliminating sickness and disease, and in prolonging the longevity of life. One can only imagine the feeling of an individual who is told that he or she has a rare, incurable disease without hope of a chance to live. This fear and confusion you would not wish upon anyone. On learning of this devastating reality, all we can do is keep on praying and believing that in time, salvation and a new beginning will arise.

A Special Day

Valentine's Day is a special occasion each year when couples renew their vows of love, commitment, and dedication. We celebrate this day to realize and appreciate the close mutual bond that is nurtured and preserved to foster a lasting and loving relationship. We must remember never to neglect the needs and wants of the person we cherish. Always express compassion and support, be faithful and trustworthy toward each other, and your life will be full of joy, happiness, and love.

Overcome Your Setbacks

I know that you are experiencing pain at times because of uncertainty, but with God's help, you will overcome your setbacks and become a stronger person for it. No matter what obstacles have gotten in your way over life's existence, we are a family who must stay together and support each other. We must always make a special effort to try to understand one another no matter what our point of view is.

With God's Help

I know that you are experiencing pain at times because of uncertainty, but with God's help, you will overcome your setbacks and become a stronger person for them. No matter what obstacles have gotten in your way over life's existence, we are a family who must join together and support each other. We must always make a special effort to try to understand one another no matter what our point of view, even when we disagree.

Why Me?

I wish I can stay young forever and live free from all misery in my body and mind. As time goes by, I will have to face the certainty of challenging the weaknesses to which my body will surrender. When I become a victim of physical afflictions, I pray to the Lord for strength, courage, and freedom from the burdens of my illness. The Lord above will make the final decision no matter how hard I pray and beg for mercy with my heart and soul to overcome the pain and suffering.

A Prayer For Sight

As a blind person, I ask myself why I wasn't given the opportunity to be able to see the world and all its beauty. I ask my creator to allow me to understand why others see when I don't have the chance to see the stars, the sun, and the moon. Although I know that I am not alone in not seeing the world, I still ask myself why I was chosen to live in darkness and not see the light of day. Deep down inside, I pray that God will give me the gift of vision, for I am innocent and can only hope that the gracious Lord will grant me this wish. All I can do now is hope and pray that my reward in my new life will be that I will be able to see for the first time.

Why So Soon?

I could never imagine that I could live without your love. I believed you when you told me you would never leave me. We worked so hard to create a beautiful relationship together. One day I will understand why the Lord decided to take you from me so soon.

Show Your Spirit

Focus on who you are and what you can be. You have strengths you must see. Focus on your weaknesses and take control. Show your spirit and loving soul. Thank the heavens and have no fear. You are a blessed child; make your life a success. You are put to the test each and every day; it is up to you to choose the way. Have no doubt, go forward, and believe. Take a path and you will succeed. See the beauty within and all you can be. Dwell not on your pain but feel the suffering of others. Understand the love around you and that your life is part of God's plan.

Your Tender Mercy

Put yourself in the place of a family suffering with and caring for a child who has little hope of enjoying a full and satisfying life. To endure this pain and uncertainty, you must cling to hope and have faith that God will provide the answer to why certain children are denied a normal and healthy life. I know I am not alone and ask for your tender mercy that you spare all your children and give them a life as you have given me.

Death From Fire

No living life form could ever imagine death by fire. Although we all think about the pain and agony in one's human body, envision the chaos and panic when a body is being consumed by a powerful man-made force and disaster. Countless lives have been destroyed or disfigured by fire either through war, accidents, or intentional acts of evil. We should pause to reflect upon the lost souls, many of whom were innocent children who suffered a horrible, agonizing demise. We must hope and ask our Heavenly Father to protect us from such a fate of death from fire.

What Is Faith?

Faith is a powerful force within us that gives us a sense of direction and hope in the afterlife. Without faith, there is no peace of mind and only confusion, which will cause you to lose sight of your determination and principles. Faith plays an important role in guiding you and will provide strength and meaning in your life. With this strong feeling within you, you will be able to believe in the afterlife after your demise.

VI

September 11, 2001

TO OUR POLICE OFFICERS, FIREFIGHTERS, EMERGENCY TECHNICIANS, AND PORT AUTHORITY OFFICERS

You sacrificed your lives with acts of courage and bravery to save others on the morning of September 11, 2001. Your unselfish heroism was unparalleled and must be recognized as an everlasting monument to the victims and their families. Your dedication and accomplishments strengthened and encouraged us to understand those events, which forever changed our lives.

As the city mourns its loss, your efforts to heal our wounds continue to give us hope. We pray that the Lord bless you and your families with His graciousness and reward you with His understanding, love, sympathy, and patience. Your fearlessness and perseverance alleviate the pain our lives have accepted, and you have succeeded triumphantly.

Our faith in you allows us to realize that all life is precious and invaluable to each and every one of us. History will demonstrate that this was your defining moment, which will forever be remembered as one of the most unforeseen and horrific tragedies to challenge our nation. We thank our firefighters, police officers, emergency technicians and Port Authority officers, who are an inspiration to all Americans.

A poetic reminder of the 9/11/01 tragedy to memorialize our heroes' dedication and ultimate sacrifice.

How Is It Possible

Tribute to September 11, 2001

Family and Friends Who Perished

How is it possible you are no longer in my life? You left me suddenly without saying goodbye. How is it possible to foresee a new dawn? Your memories keep my faith alive. How is it possible to live without your touch, your smile, and your love?

How is it possible to flourish in your absence? The thought of being forever alone makes my life uncertain. How is it possible this unforeseen attack has erased our hopes and dreams? I pray for strength and that the Lord usher me through the dark days and lonely nights. God only knows the reasons and meaning behind his actions.

How is it possible to find acceptance and endure this pain? You loved me, cherished me, enriched me, and protected me. How is it possible that our love was divided forever? Our love was meant to last a lifetime. How is it possible to envision you as an angel with the Lord? How is it possible?

Exemplary Father And Dedicated Husband, 9/11

In my lifetime, I have been privileged to have met the most admirable and wonderful human being, who truly inspired me to see the goodness in all people. My husband was such a person, and he will be remembered by me and my family forever. He was an exemplary father, a dedicated husband, and a friend to all who knew him. He will be deeply missed, and I pray that he is happy in heaven, watching down upon all of his family and friends. He always took that extra step to make you laugh when you were sad. He would cry with you to accompany you in your pain and suffering, and he always expressed his love and passion for others. There is not a day that goes by that my true love is not remembered and appreciated for all the good deeds he accomplished and the acts of kindness he performed for his family and friends. May he rest in eternal peace, and we will always keep him in our hearts. I pray for strength and that the Lord usher me through the dark days and lonely nights that I must endure.

To the Men and Women of our Armed Services

As a nation, each and every citizen must truly understand the unending dedication and sacrifice which is made by our young men and women who serve to protect us from threats both foreign and domestic. They offer their lives in order to preserve our freedom and way of life. We must always keep them in our thoughts and prayers never forgetting the scars of war which took their lives and caused permanent physical and mental wounds. We pray to the lord that their souls rest in peace. We must keep them in our vision and they will recognize that their memory will never be forgotten. We must always pray for them and appreciate them for their duty, honor and courage.

Freedom For Iraq and Afghanistan

Our military forces and the American people ensure that our values and freedom are preserved, protected, and preferred for all nations who want freedom, justice, and happiness. America's fighting men and women have shown their bravery and determination in achieving a glorious victory for the people of Iraq who have been suppressed for decades. That accomplishment will forever be recognized and remembered as the true example of leadership for world peace and salvation. All countries are safer and secure because of that great triumph of military might to attain unity, harmony, and justice for all mankind who suffer such a fate. We pray for the warriors' safe return to their families and loved ones, and we thank them all for their valor.

*This book is dedicated to my mother, Madeline
and my fanther, Luke*

*I dedicate this beautiful inspirational work to my beloved mother,
Madeline, who passed away on June 3, 2014. My mother was a strong
and wonderful woman who provided me with a loving and positive view
of the world. She encouraged me to create and write the enlightening
poems, poetry, and musical compositions that accompany this work of
art. The opportunity that was given to me was supported by the strong
leadership provided by my father, Luke Gasparre Sr., a WWII veteran who
fought in the Battle of the Bulge. He continues to be an inspiration to
me and my family, and he was instrumental as a creative and talented
force in my life. At the age of 95, he represents remarkable leadership
qualities and a devotion to his family. Most important to me, I was gifted
with having three precious children whom I nurtured and cared for, and
I had the privilege of always being there for them, creating a permanent
and loving bond. I wish to pay special tribute to my sister Rose Ann, who
has always been there for me through good and bad times. She plays
an important role, especially after our mother's passing, in keeping our
family strong and united. I'm so grateful to have such a loving family
behind me and the spiritual presence of my mother who continues to
influence my writings and life's philosophy.*

October is National Breast Cancer Awareness Month

I hope I am never exposed to breast cancer. But this could happen to you or to anyone of us. Understand how serious this disease can be. It has resulted in the loss of countless lives and serious hardships to families, friends, and loved ones. We must all come together to remember those who have suffered and are continuing to suffer from this devastating and horrible sickness.

As a woman, you should understand and be aware of the serious risk of breast cancer. If you know someone who is a breast cancer survivor or someone who was unable to defeat or overcome this devastating cancer, we must always be mindful of their suffering and never give up in the search to eliminate breast cancer from our world. Always keep a place in your heart and remember them for who they were.

Lasting Thoughts

Hatred in the heart is caused by fear of our differences. The drip of hatred can only be cured by love.

§

Do not judge from without but judge from within and learn to appreciate your individuality.

§

Don't let evil win, find a way to defeat and overcome it.

§

Take time out and you will feel the difference in your life.

§

Don't criticize others examine who you are and what you believe in.

§

Leave your troubles behind and start a new day, fresh in the hope of discovering your new potential.

§

Be courageous and you will succeed.

§

Life can be difficult if you allow it to be so.

§

Lasting Thoughts

There is another heart out there even after a broken heart.

§

Rise above your challenges and be who you are.

§

To improve one's image look in the mirror and relate to yourself.

§

Lift your sights and surround yourself with positive and successful role

models. Then you will see that your life has meaning.

§

When you are lost in your thoughts express yourself and you will feel

cleansed and purified.

§

I can see through water but I cannot see through you.

§

Saying I love you are only words unless and until I show you my love.

The flowers I gave you may die but my love for you will last a life time.

§

Find a way to discover new opportunities to improve your life. Do not

be afraid to fail. Use all your strengths and means to confront your

fears

Lasting Thoughts

Find a way to discover new opportunities to improve your life. Do not be afraid to fail. Use all your strengths and means to confront your fears and to rise above the confusion that lies in your state of mind. Then you will achieve freedom and peace in your heart and soul.

§

Stand up for what you believe in. Express who you are, and let no heartache keep you from your dreams and potential.

§

When love starts fading in your life, you will feel emptiness within. Do not retreat into your loneliness but find a way to love again.

§

Nothing stays the same. Learn to let go of your past, and embrace the future.

§

Keep your memories in your heart, and the love that you share will make all the difference.

§

Life is special to those who welcome changes.

Do not fear change but embrace it with courage and passion.

Lasting Thoughts

Don't be weak-minded.

Show strength of character, and rise above your confusion.

§

Find a way to make a difference in someone's life.

§

Deep within the clouds are raindrops of love. The purity that flows from above will cleanse your heart and soul.

§

When you live in darkness, you are lost and unable to find your way. The truth is within you, so find the light.

§

Tell her how you feel before she slips away. You may never have a chance to say goodbye, so tell her you love her.

§

Living behind four walls closes your mind and prevents you from seeing beyond your imagination. Open the door, and let freedom in.

§

Ignore all the drama around you.

Focus instead on what is important and meaningful in your life.

Lasting Thoughts

When you are feeling down and alone, share your feelings, and do not be afraid of the truth.

§

When the curtain closes, the show is over. Fulfill every hope and desire because your life is limited and time is precious.

§

I look out the window, and day becomes night. My vision of you is lost from my sight. I must wait for a new day and hope you care to join me so I do not despair.

§

Open your heart, and let love in.

§

Every day I see you is another day of pleasure.

§

Building trust takes time with the ones you love.

§

Be patient with others, and do not rush to judgment.

§

Every picture tells a story. Your story can be next.

Lasting Thoughts

It is important to care for others, but you are the one who must remain stable and healthy.

§

Surround yourself with those who represent honesty and success in all they do.

§

Show compassion in your journey through life.

§

Everyone needs a helping hand, so we must reach out to one another.

§

The smallest thing can make a difference in someone's life.

§

When I see your precious smile, I now realize that you are the piece that completes my puzzle. Now I know how much you mean to me.

§

It will take time for you to discover who you really are. Be patient, and your time will come.

§

Don't wait for your light to go out. Change your life today to capture tomorrow.

Lasting Thoughts

Look beyond your dreams, and capture your moment in time.

§

The truth is within you, so be honest with yourself.

§

Be who you are, and allow yourself to rejoice.

§

Accept yourself, and never look back at what could have been. You are beautiful as you are.

§

Life is a challenge, so stand up to it, and save yourself.

§

Give to others to help them feel wanted.

§

Decide to do something positive.

§

I promise to give you my soul only if you will give me your heart.

§

Show support to those who are hurting.

§

Everyone deserves a second chance, so forgive always.

Lasting Thoughts

Holding onto anger will destroy your soul.

§

Don't look back in anger. Look beyond today.

§

Show leadership, and help others.

§

Words of kindness will comfort the lonely.

§

A kind word to someone will always be remembered.

§

Being in love is a special gift. Give of yourself to the one you love.

§

Open your heart, and let love into your life. You may find it when you least expect it.

§

Love may grow if you have the same feelings for each other.

§

Plant the seed of love, and hope it blossoms in your favor.

Lasting Thoughts

Happiness is not gained by winning alone but by commitment and determination.

§

Everything in life is temporary. So hold on to what is meaningful to you.

§

It's not what you have but what you are to others.

§

Happiness is the joy of family and friends. Show compassion, and appreciate who they are

§

When love fails you, do not despair. With time, you will love again.

§

When there is hurt and sorrow in your life, find someone who will comfort you and ease the pain.

§

Little expressions of love can win a person's heart.

§

Giving time to another creates moments of love.

Lasting Thoughts

Look beyond today, and the possibilities will be endless.

§

Yesterday is gone, and a new day has arrived.

§

Bitter times can teach and make us grow.

§

Hard times build character.

§

Only when you fail can you appreciate success.

§

A book cover tells only part of your story. What's inside belongs to you.

§

A world without you is a world without love.

§

A clear mind will give you a vision of hope.

§

Reach beyond your limits. Stay true to yourself.

Lasting Thoughts

When the dust settles, your life will be visible.

§

What matters is what's in your heart.

§

Being grateful about who you are will make a difference in what you are.

§

Your shadow is a reflection of you. It's part of who you are.

§

Never compromise with love.

§

Let your conscience guide you, and you will never go wrong.

§

Do not abandon the truth that lies within you.

§

Live in the moment, and enjoy who you are.

§

Be a uniter, not a divider.

Lasting Thoughts

When you feel that your life is falling apart, reach out, and take someone's hand.

§

You may be wrong but have no doubt.

§

Believe in your ability to conquer your uncertainty.

§

Love conquers hate. So keep the faith, and believe in the power of love.

§

Be thankful for the love that was given to you. Love is a gift that will last forever.

§

Do not fear love; it's always in you. Express it.

§

Make someone feel wanted by giving to others.

§

Decide to do something positive.

§

Everyone deserves a second chance, so forgive and forget.

Lasting Thoughts

Look within your soul to express what you really feel.

§

I only know that I don't have you in my life another day.

§

Conquer your dreams, and you will overcome your fears.

§

Hatred in the heart is caused by fear of our differences. The drip of hatred can only be cured by love.

§

Do not judge from without, but judge from within. Learn to appreciate your individuality.

§

Don't let evil win. Find a way to defeat and overcome it.

§

Take time out, and you will feel the difference in your life.

§

Don't criticize others. Examine who you are and what you believe in.

§

Leave your troubles behind, and start a new day, fresh in the hope of discovering your new potential.

Lasting Thoughts

Be courageous, and you will succeed.

§

Life can be difficult if you allow it to be.

§

Rise above your challenges, and be who you are.

§

Find a way to discover new opportunities to improve your life.

§

Do not be afraid to fail. Use all of your strengths and means to confront your fears and rise above the confusion that lies in your mind. Then you will achieve freedom and peace in your heart and soul.

§

To improve your self-image, look in the mirror, and show more compassion and understanding to others.

§

Lift your sights, and surround yourself with positive and successful role models. Then you will see that your life has meaning.

§

When you are lost in your thoughts, express yourself, and you will feel cleansed and purified.

Lasting Thoughts

I can see through water, but I cannot see through you.

§

"I love you" are only words unless and until I show you my love.

§

The flowers I gave you may die, but my love for you will last a lifetime.

§

You have the power within you to be happy. What's holding you back?

§

Reach out to me, and I will be there for you. Trust in me, and I will never hurt you.

§

Thinking of you is like being in heaven. I want you more than ever. So come to me, and I will share my heart with you forever.

§

If you are living in the past, set yourself free. I have the key if you want to be with me.

ABOUT THE AUTHOR

Mr. Luke John Gasparre is a distinguished writer, poet, and musician who has produced a masterpiece of beautifully enhanced motivational words of inspirational insight into oneself and the reason that was given to you. As you read these words of wisdom, you will immediately be propelled into the author's mind and understand his beautiful intentions on various subjects to comfort you and reduce the stress found in our world today. You will also experience the beautiful musical compositions Mr. Gasparre has created to accompany you when you are reading these words of wisdom.

The purpose of these writings is to offer readers in one book reflections of the mind and imagination to encourage the spirit and to relieve pain and suffering in their lives. The author's poems and prayers offer a vision and direction that will make you appreciate the value of life, and they offer meaningful understanding into the mind, soul, and heart of the reader. Each expression will lift you up and provide you with practical knowledge and spiritual awareness that will be helpful to you and your loved ones.

Printed in the United States of America

Third edition December 2020

Listen to the soundtrack and more at www.21stcenturythoughts.com. On Youtube search "Luke John Gasparre".

Deep Within Your Heart

All the simple things in life can be achieved and bring happiness to your soul. But you have to imagine a vision of love before you can experience that happiness. So much time and energy is spent on improving our status in life that we lose sight of what's really important. Your life's journey will succeed when you realize the true meaning that lies deep within your heart.

www.ingramcontent.com/pod-product-compliance
Lightning Source LLC
Chambersburg PA
CBHW080058280326
41934CB00014B/3362